Invizikids

By

Mike Hallowell

Typeset by Jonathan Downes, Copyproofed by Guin Palmer.
Thanks to Bob Trubshawe
Cover and Layout by SPiderKaT for CFZ Communications
Using Microsoft Word 2000, Microsoft Publisher 2000, Adobe Photoshop CS.

First published in Great Britain by CFZ Press

CFZ Press
Myrtle Cottage
Woolsery
Bideford
North Devon
EX39 5QR

© CFZ MMXXII

ISBN: 978-1-909488-67-0

To

Maureen and Elizabeth
who were always there for me
even when they weren't

Note to the 2002 edition

Dear friends,

I remember well the day that Mike Hallowell sent me this manuscript, how impressed I was, and how disappointed I was that he had already sold publishing rights. 15 years on, give or take a week or two, and Mike and his original publisher have very kindly signed over the rights to us. I cannot recommend this book highly enough. It is, in my humble opinion, one of the best books that we have ever published, and, indeed, one of the best books ever written a Fortean subject.

Jon Downes,
April 10, 2022

Foreword

All good stories should begin with the word 'once upon a time', and I would love to begin this foreword by writing 'once upon a time when I was a little boy I had an imaginary friend, but I can't. Because I didn't. Or - to be more truthful - until I read Mike Hallowell's remarkable book I didn't think that I did. However, when I was a little boy in the Hong Kong of the 1960s, when it was still the last, lustrous jewel in the crown of an Empire on which the Sun never set, my friend Jonathan Halbert and I did have an imaginary car. Today is the first time I've even thought of Jonathan Halbert for about 40 years. His parents moved back to England, and as far as I know, I last saw him in the summer of 1966. I wonder what he's doing now, whether he has forgotten me like I had forgotten him, and whether he too has 'CaseCar' as a relict, phantom memory in the deepest recesses of his psyche.

CaseCar was a peculiar vehicle, like a elongated flatbed truck, low on the ground with an exhaust pipe like a silver chimney attached vertically into the side of the cab. I don't know who drove CaseCar. It wasn't me or Jonathan, but he (I know he was male in gender, don't ask me how) certainly existed, and the three of us had various adventures, and on some occasions he got us both into trouble. Whenever I had committed some particularly egregious crime, it was CaseCar's fault, and although my parents both used to chastise me for blaming something that didn't exist, with the wisdom of four decades hindsight I'm certain that, for me and Jonathan at least, CaseCar had some sort of objective reality. I cannot remember much more about him; indeed my only memories are of the aforesaid chastisement, and of being told to 'shut up and stop jabbering on about bloody CaseCar all the time' by a frustrated Paterfamilias. All this came flooding back when I read Mike's description of 'animates' – non-human or imaginary animal imaginary friends.

A few years later when I had reached the exalted age of nine or ten, my little brother Richard, (now a retired high-ranking army chaplain) had a number of playmates from amongst the faerie folk. I wonder if he remembers them now, and if so how he reconciles that memory with the lifepath of his adulthood.

In 2000 I went to London to attend a concert by legendary rock musician Pete Townshend who was showcasing songs from this even more legendary music project 'Lifehouse'. Townshend explains the story:

"The essence of the storyline is a kind of futuristic scene. It's a fantasy set at a time when rock 'n' roll didn't exist. The world is completely collapsing and the only experience anybody ever had was through test tubes. They lived the TV programmes, in a way. Everything was programmed. They were enemies with people who gave us entertainment intravenously, and the heroes were savages who kept rock 'n' roll as a primitive force and had gone to live with it in the woods. The story was about these two sides coming together for a brief battle."

The story has been kicking around since about 1970, and was originally mooted as an album and a film by Townshend's band The Who. It never materialised, although Townshend has periodically revisited this concept ever since. To date the most concrete realisation of the project was in a BBC radio play in 1999, set on Millennium Eve.

The main protagonist of the story is Ray High, a troubled ex-rock singer obviously based on Townshend himself. In the 1999 play Ray and Sally are farmers who grow, as Sally said, 'dead potatoes'. Their daughter Mary runs away from home to visit a hacker who has fascinated her with pirate radio advertisements. Ray goes to try to find his lost child, along the way meeting his childhood self, Rayboy, and his imaginary friend The Caretaker. Townshend's exploration of the need for an imaginary friend, and his exploration of the concept of what would happen when a childhood imaginary friend turns up in adult life, opens an extraordinary can of worms. This is not the time nor the place for scholarly discussion of similar themes within Townshend's work, but even a song like 'Dr Jimmy and Mr Jim' from Quadrophenia when he discusses a character who 'only comes out when I drink my gin', and Whiskey Man (by his deceased bandmate John Entwistle), something that seem to be a clumsy description of bad behaviour caused by drunkenness can suddenly be seen in a whole new light when one looks of the story of Ray High and his imaginary friend.

I know many adult people who imbue their pets with characteristics that only they can see. I admit that I am one of those sad individuals. Perhaps as adults we no longer allow our imaginary friends from childhood to enter into our waking moments, but – instead – replace them with bizarrely anthropomorphised versions of our domestic pets, whose invented characteristics are very real to us. I know I do.

Mike Hallowell has written a remarkable book which – to the best of my knowledge – is the first of its kind. I think that he should be congratulated for his extremely hard work that this research must've taken, but I feel I should warn him. If this book becomes as popular as it deserves, he is going to be inundated with personal accounts of imaginary friends. I foresee a steady stream of sequels stretching on until he is in his dotage.

Sorry. I have to go. I can hear CaseCar trundling down the drive.

Slainte,

Jon Downes,
The Centre for Fortean Zoology,
Myrtle Cottage,
Woolfardisworthy,
Bideford, North Devon
EX39 5QR

March, 2007

Introduction

Once upon a time I used to live in a safe world, a world in which everything made sense and always seemed to work out. As a child I was surrounded by things eternal; a father who always came home from work at 6 p.m., a mother who always cooked my meals and a toy box that was always filled with a changing but incredibly entrancing selection of things to play with.

My childhood innocence blinded me to the fact that things would change. I never envisaged that, at some far-off, future time, my mother and father would divorce and my toy box would play host to an assortment of drills, hammers, chisels and other tools.

When Maureen arrived on the scene I was still innocent.

I can't remember exactly when she first appeared, but I can certainly remember where. It was in the kitchen of my parents' first floor flat in Park Road, Hebburn, in the County of Tyne and Wear; except then it was in the County of Durham, before the boundaries changed.

I was standing in the kitchen looking towards the bathroom. It was a strange bathroom, actually, as it didn't contain a bath. It was only five feet in length and just over three feet in width, and the only thing it contained was a toilet. Back in the late fifties it wasn't deemed polite to refer to the toilet *as* a toilet. You could call it a WC or a bathroom, though, even if you didn't have a bath.

But I digress. The walls of the kitchen were covered in an insipid green emulsion paint; very modern, very fifties. There was a vegetable rack in the corner, and I remember enjoying the damp, earthy smell of the King Edward potatoes and cabbages that nestled therein.

There was also a kitchen table and four chairs. The frames were tubular steel and the seats were covered in yellow and blue vinyl. None of your old-fashioned leather; Mum and dad were going up in the world, and could now afford *real vinyl*. Well, it was a fifties' thing.

What I was doing or where I was going is now obscured by time's gentle fog. Maybe I intended to pay a visit to the 'bathroom', who

The Author aged Three

knows. In any event, she suddenly appeared and frightened the living daylights out of me. She was small, elfin-faced – almost urchin-like. Her blonde-cum-chestnut hair was unkempt, and I remember little about her clothes other than that they were plain and unassuming. What little I can recall will be brought to light in a later chapter.

She turned her head on one side and stared at me curiously. Her blue eyes were piercing, inquisitive.

> 'Hello. My name's Maureen and I want to be your friend'.

And so it was that Maureen, seemingly out of the ether, arrived. Never for a moment did I question who she was, from whence she came or how she had turned up at Park Road in Hebburn. Wrapped in a blanket of childish innocence I simply accepted that Maureen now lived in our house, and from that day forth she became a regular companion; my *only* regular companion, in fact. We hid in cupboards together and giggled. We bounced up and down on the bloc coloured moquette sofa when mum wasn't looking, rolled my red, plastic ball back and forth and ran from room to room like lunatics playing catch-me-if-you-can. They were happy, carefree days.

I was only a toddler at the time, but nevertheless I became dimly aware, at some point, that something wasn't quite right. Why didn't my mother ever talk to Maureen? Why did Maureen sometimes have to stand at the side of the table and watch as we ate, unless I specifically asked my mother to set a place for her? Why didn't my father acknowledge her, either? I wanted to say something, but wasn't sure exactly what. And then, one day, Maureen got upset. I wasn't sure why, and didn't have the time to figure it out. I was too busy playing with my model multi-storey car park and petrol station and trying to figure out why the house was in such a mess. There were cardboard boxes and wooden tea chests everywhere, and all my family's worldly goods were being systematically placed in them.

Two days later we moved, and then I knew why Maureen had been upset. Her tears had been shed because she knew we would never see each other again. I was upset too; I really liked Maureen.

Our flat in Armstrong Terrace, South Shields, was much the same as the one we had left. Except it was bigger. Maureen faded from my mind, and I concentrated on navigating my way around our new home.

Robert, my cousin, was several years older than I was. He had graduated from toyhood, and was now allowed to play outdoors with friends. This meant that the toy zoo which my aunt had bought him was now gathering dust in a cupboard. She wanted rid of it, and fortunately I was the grateful inheritor of a large box full of die-cast metal animals, keepers, buildings and railings. While my mother and her sister chatted in the kitchen, I set about erecting a massive animal sanctuary in the centre of the living-room carpet. Or at least I would have, if I could have figured out how to clip the sections of fencing together.

And this is where Elizabeth entered the picture. Suddenly she was sitting opposite and saying, 'Here, I'll show you how to do it'. I watched, with not the slightest degree of surprise at her unannounced appearance, as she proceeded to build my zoo for me. And then she smiled and went away.

ned into months, I began to notice a similar pattern.
ignoring Elizabeth too. And neither was she allowed
And so, one summer's day as my mother prepared
1at a place be set for Elizabeth. My mother – merely
..g a childish fantasy, as she thought – agreed. That evening
Elizabeth sat with us and dined on whatever it was we ate. If my
memory serves me correctly it was fish fingers. I was happy.

Maureen had been mischievous and excitable. She made my heart
beat. She was naughty, but loveable. Elizabeth, on the other hand, was
of a different social stratum altogether. She dressed in expensive silk
frocks with large ribbons, and her blonde hair was always perfectly
drawn back over her scalp into a vivacious ponytail. She was friendly,
but cultured like Lewis Carroll's *Alice*. She had the knack of getting her
own way, quietly but firmly, and yet without making you feel
oppressed. I was in awe of Elizabeth.

At the age of eight we moved again, and – just like Maureen –
Elizabeth dissipated from my consciousness and plunged herself into
the farthest reaches of my cerebellum. I made other friends, but never
completely forgot my two ethereal companions.

As a journalist who specialises in writing about paranormal
phenomena, I have built up an increasing number of case files
concerning youngsters who, like me, enjoyed the strange but welcome
presence of an 'invisible friend'; invisible, that is, to anyone other than
ourselves.

Such invisible companions are hard to quantify. They enter our reality
and depart from it with ease. In my experience at least, they seem to be
bound to a fixed geographical location.

Bizarrely, I could actually see my friends eating food which my mother
set out for them, while my mother's perception was that the food was
left on the plate. This has forced me to consider the even stranger
possibility that, at least at mealtimes, my mother and I were in the
same place and time, but simultaneously experiencing two slightly
differing realities – one in which the food was eaten and one in which
it stayed untouched. How, then, was I sharing *my* reality with a mother
who apparently belonged to a different time-line in which the food
was eaten? If this mother was from a different reality, what was she
doing in mine, and why could she not see that the food had *been*
eaten? And where was the 'real' mother from the reality that I was
currently experiencing?

The questions multiply as fast as they are asked, and it is difficult indeed to fit potential answers into a coherent philosophical or scientific framework.

Some time ago, someone asked me if I'd ever had an imaginary friend as a child. Suddenly, a veritable cornucopia of happy but largely buried memories flooded out. Maureen and Elizabeth had been resurrected. I no longer see them, but my memories are clear. I inhabit a world which offers – at least as far as I am aware – no easy access to other dimensional realities. My childhood companions are not so bound, and I cannot help but feel that they still exist in some place and in some time. I doubt that I shall ever see them again, but I remember them fondly.

In this book I aim to explore the strange phenomenon of 'invisible' childhood companions. You will come to see, as did I, that it is far more complex than it at first appears. There is more than one kind of companion, and each kind seems to have its own, subtle subculture. Sometimes these types are so different that it could be argued that they are entirely different phenomena altogether. However, they are often connected by subtle common denominators that suggest a definite link.

This volume is not a scientific treatise. I have not employed scientific methodology in my research, firstly, because I am not trained to do so, and secondly because I am not trying to convince the scientific establishment that 'invisible' childhood companions really exist. This book is for those who are curious about the subject matter and who can read the contents with a degree of common sense. I have relied purely on my skills as an investigative writer, and if some find this insufficient then I apologise in advance.

In June 2006, I was asked to speak at a conference on this subject, and someone in the audience asked me what, in my opinion, the most bizarre aspect of this strange phenomenon was. My answer probably surprised a few people. Of course, the phenomenon itself is fascinating, but more intriguing still is the reaction of most people to it. Let me explain why.

If the average person in the street came to believe that their home was infested by a poltergeist – whatever or whoever a poltergeist may be – their reaction would normally be one of alarm or even naked, unvarnished fear. The idea that an invisible entity is stalking their dwelling, moving furniture, turning taps on and off and making strange noises in the dead of night, is a thought veritably guaranteed to dissipate calm. However, parents of children who claim to have 'invisible' childhood friends show no such consternation. Their child is apparently interacting with an invisible entity of sorts – an entity who is engaging their son or daughter in conversation and manipulating their behaviour – and yet they most often just shrug their shoulders. Adults who talk to invisible people are labelled mentally ill, but children who do the self-same thing nary raise an eyebrow.

Of course, it could be argued that parents do not really believe that the 'invisible' friends exist. But even so, shouldn't it be disturbing to them that their children are speaking on a regular basis to someone or something that isn't really there? Rather than drag their child off to the doctor, most parents are quite content just to let the situation perpetuate. Perhaps there is something inside the human consciousness that prevents us from panicking, something which tells us that 'invisible' childhood friends are no threat to either the young experient and/or their family.

I have Native American heritage, and, because I take both the cultural and spiritual side of my life very seriously, I tend to look at the world differently. I see things as I have been trained to see them; through Indian eyes. I mention this because, in my experience, Native Americans are far better equipped psychologically, emotionally and spiritually to deal with this type of phenomenon than those raised in a 'European' cultural environment which, despite its ostensible open-mindedness, is still extremely sceptical towards the idea that quasi-corporeal entities of any kind can really exist.

I do not have all the answers to this strange phenomenon, but I have answers of sorts with which I am content. These are, it is true, answers borne on the wings of my Indian culture, but I think they would largely satisfy those of European or non-Indian heritage too. I will return to this aspect of my research later.

John A. Wheeler once said, 'If you haven't found something strange during the day, it hasn't been much of a day.' The phenomenon of 'invisible' childhood friends speaks realms about the truth behind this maxim.

Michael J. Hallowell

West Boldon
March 2007

A word about nomenclature

The phenomenon at the heart of this volume is normally referred to as that of 'invisible childhood friends' or 'imaginary childhood friends'. However, even a cursory examination will show that these descriptions are unsatisfactory. Let me explain why.

Firstly, they both make a huge assumption regarding the nature of the phenomenon in question; specifically, that the 'entities' are either imaginary and/ or invisible. In this book I will cast doubt upon the notion that they are merely the product of an over-active imagination. There is substantial circumstantial evidence that, at least on some objective level, they really do exist. Secondly, as I have already pointed out, they may be invisible to bystanders but they are most certainly not invisible to the experients

The word 'friend' is also problematical, for this suggests that the relationship between an experient and an entity is always benign. True, this is almost always the case, but some entities of this nature, although non-threatening, are not exactly 'friendly' in the normal sense of the word.

Throughout this book I will, therefore, refer to these entities as 'Quasi-Corporeal Companions' or 'QCCs' for short. 'Quasi-corporeal' because the entities cannot really be described as 'non-corporeal'; a term I once employed, but have now abandoned. To experients, the entities in question are as solid – 'real' – as you and I. I choose to use the word 'companion' because the word is both less intimate and less 'loaded' than the term 'friend'.

~~~~~~~

A small number of experients did not wish for their real names to be used in this book. In such cases, the pseudonyms used have been suffixed with an asterisk, thus – * – at their first appearance.

~~~~~~~

Chapter one

Catch...

For nearly a decade I have penned a column for the UK's oldest provincial newspaper, the *Shields Gazette.* The column, *Bizarre*, is essentially a potpourri of paranormal phenomena. Readers send me details of ghost stories, UFO sightings and a host of strange experiences and delight at seeing them in print. Writing *Bizarre* is a labour of love.

In March 2000, I received a letter from a reader called John Tatters, a retired tailor from Birmingham who has spent many years in Iceland. John recalled that his son had an 'invisible friend' when he was a toddler during the 1940s. When the toddler kept mentioning 'Stephen' he laughed at first, but then a strange experience made him think again.

One day, his son was throwing a football around in the garden of their home. At some point the child threw the ball towards a large rhododendron bush, and John realised that he must have been playing with 'the invisible friend', for he heard him shout, 'Here Stephen... catch!' He was not prepared for what happened next.

'I swear down that the ball seemed to stop in mid-air by the bush and then sail back across the garden towards my son, as if thrown by an invisible pair of hands. He missed the ball, and then shouted, 'Try again, Stephen!' But I wasn't having any of it. I dragged him inside like a shot and told him never to mention 'Stephen' again. He never did, but told me later that he resented the way I'd forced his friend to go away.'

When I was a child I had an almost identical experience. My maternal grandmother was babysitting me, and had gone into the kitchen to make a cup of tea. Elizabeth appeared and we began to roll a red, plastic ball back and forth across the living room floor between us.

Suddenly my grandmother entered the room
invisible to my grandmother – rolled the ball I
remember the look of astonishment on her fa<
back out into the kitchen and never said ar
matter. This wasn't the first time that an 'imagir
consternation in the presence of my grandmc
the last.

John's tale intrigued me, and I decided to publish it in *Bizarre*. It
appeared in the *Gazette* on Thursday April 4, 2000, and generated a
considerable response. I concluded the article by posing some
questions to readers:

> There are some peculiarities about 'invisible' childhood
> companions which we do not understand. They seem,
> for instance, to be tied to a fixed geographical location.
> When a family moves home their child's invisible
> companion – if he or she has one – will almost certainly
> stay put. This characteristic seems to strengthen the
> theory that these apparitions are probably some type of
> ghost, for ghosts are also bound to certain geographical
> areas and do not normally follow you around.
>
> Many people are embarrassed to admit that they once
> had an 'invisible' childhood companion, scared that
> people will think they are mentally unbalanced. This is
> nonsense. If this phenomenon is simply the product of a
> creative imagination, then it is nothing to worry about.
>
> But what if the opposite is true? What if these strange
> entities are in some sense real, perhaps opening up
> doorways to a dimension of existence that we know
> little or nothing about? Well, I wouldn't worry about it.
> I've never heard of anyone ever being terrified by an
> 'invisible childhood companion'. Whatever they are,
> they seem to be benign, enriching the lives of the 'real'
> children they play with.

The letters and emails I received from readers prompted me to think
further about the phenomenon. With hindsight I now know that I was
too hasty by far in concluding that QCCs were 'probably some type of
ghost'. Whatever they are, they represent a complex phenomenon that
likely has little to do with apparitions or hauntings, at least in the
conventional sense.

me time pondering over my own experiences as a child. aureen and Elizabeth seemed real? No; they *were* real; real in that may differ from the normal definition of the word, but real etheless.

decided to dig deeper.

Chapter two

Cosmic connections

In May 2000, not long after I detailed John Tatters's experience in my *Shields Gazette* column, I received an email from Donna Kent. Donna is president of *the Cosmic Society of Paranormal Investigation* in the USA, and has appeared on numerous television programmes connected with what we may generically call 'the unexplained'.

Let me say something about Donna. She possesses an enthusiasm for her craft that is almost electric and once she gets her teeth into something she inevitably sticks with the programme. She certainly believes that that there's something in paranormal phenomena, and she isn't going to let go until she's got to the bottom of it. The *Cosmic Connections* website is not a highbrow environment for those who want to debate the more philosophical issues surrounding paranormal research. Members of *Cosmic Connections* seem to prefer to do that in person. It is primarily a users site: where to buy, what to see, when to meet. Nevertheless, it contains hundreds of photographs of allegedly paranormal phenomena, and the people at *Cosmic Connections* are probably more influential than any other group in the USA for perpetuating the interest of the average person in the street in the unknown. Somehow they manage to combine street-level presentation with nuclear-level verve, and the result is the sort of kindling that the paranormal world needs to stop the fires of common interest in the subject dying out.

At their meetings, normally held at the Carousel Gardens restaurant is Seymour, Connecticut – haunted, of course – *Cosmic Connections* have enjoyed presentations by some heavyweight speakers, including Joyce St Germaine, Roger Pyle and Robert Graham.

Back in 2000, Donna kindly asked me if I'd like to pen an article for the society's journal, also called *Cosmic Connections,* on the subject of 'imaginary' childhood friends. I agreed and the article, entitled 'True Encounters', detailed my own experiences with both Maureen and

Donna Kent

Elizabeth. Little did I know that the appearance of my article would precipitate an interest in the subject that ultimately resulted in the writing of the volume you now hold in your hands.

My contact details appeared as an appendix, and, as with my previous article in the *Shields Gazette*, it drew quite a response. Readers contacted me with their own experiences, and this only served to deepen my curiosity.

One reader, John Alvarez, related his own QCC experience:

> When I was a child I lived in New Mexico. I had three brothers and two sisters, and was basically a happy, contented youngster.
>
> One day, when I was around four years-old, I think, I was sitting in an old barn which belonged to my grandfather. Suddenly a bale of hay in the corner started to rustle as if something was inside it. I was alarmed, and concluded that it was probably a rat. I stood up and was just about to run outside when something weird happened.
>
> Suddenly the top half of a man appeared to 'explode' from the hay. He was old and wore a black hat with a wide brim. He smiled in a way that was nice and said, 'Hello, my name is Roggie-Roggie. Are you okay?'

I told him I was fine. He said, 'You know, you should
be careful when you play in the hay. Sometimes it can
be sharp and you might prick yourself.'

Without any warning he suddenly disappeared in the
hay again and I ran back to my grandfather's house.

Several things intrigued me about John's account. Firstly, the strange
way that the apparition had manifested itself to the youngster.
Secondly, the name 'Roggie-Roggie'. I did a Google search on 'Roggie-
Roggie' but met with no success. The epithet, to all intents and
purposes, seemed to be nonsensical. Later I would discover that the
name Roggie-Roggie placed the man with the big hat firmly in the
QCC category; something which I'll explain in a later chapter.

John Alvarez, for whatever reason, obviously thought that Roggie-
Roggie was a quasi-corporeal companion – why else would he have
contacted me, as his email had been prompted by my article in *Cosmic
Connections* on that very subject?

Another reader, who signed herself simply as 'NK', also told me of her
experience with a QCC.

When I was little I wasn't a very nice kid. I used to pull
the legs off bugs, steal from my mother's purse and
pinch whole packets of Twinkies from the shelf in the
kitchen. Then I'd blame my brother.

One day I was looking through my mom's pockets for
cash when my 'friend' Cody appeared. He said, 'Hey,
what are you doing? Stop that!'

Cody always used to appear when I was doing bad
stuff. He would tick me off. Sometimes he'd play with
me, though, and I liked him.

It struck me that there was a vague similarity between NK's experience
and that of John Alvarez. In both encounters, the QCC had tried to
help the young experients. Roggie-Roggie had tried to advise John in a
practical sense, warning him about the dangers of playing in the hay.
NK's friend, Cody, had tried to help NK by warning her away from
morally unacceptable behaviour. It wasn't much to go on, but it made
me wonder if both QCCs could have a common origin of sorts.

Around the same time, I had to travel to Merseyside on business for a
few days. I took the train from Newcastle Central Station to Liverpool

Lime Street, settled back in my seat and started to thumb through a novel. After a stop or two a woman got on and, after struggling to place her burgeoning luggage on the overhead rack, sat down in the seat directly opposite.

Although I made no effort to speak, it soon became evident that she didn't want to spend her journey in isolation. She asked me if I was enjoying the book I was reading. I replied in the affirmative. She wanted to know if I liked reading Catherine Cookson novels. I replied in the negative. Helpless, I found myself drawn into conversation. Once I told her that I wrote about the paranormal for a living she was fascinated. With saucer-like eyes she probed me about ghosts, the Loch Ness monster, Uri Geller and the film *Close Encounters of the Third Kind*. At some point the phenomenon of 'invisible' childhood friends entered the metaphorical arena, and the woman, who called herself Lesley, immediately told me of her sister's experience. Suddenly I was interested.

> My sister used to have one of those. It was a little girl
> called Foo-Foo. She was always talking to her, playing
> with her... she used to drive us mad. We even had to
> buy sweets for her in the supermarket.

It was the name of this particular QCC that riveted me. John Alvarez had called his QCC Roggie-Roggie. This woman's sister called her QCC Foo-Foo. It still wasn't much to 'hang my hat on' so to speak, but it struck me as odd that both experients had used what I later came to call a 'double-barrelled repetitive' when referring to their ethereal companions.

Lesley dragged her luggage off the train at Leeds, noisily berating passengers who didn't get out of the way in time. She'd been a pain in the arse in some respects, but I was glad that I'd been able to speak to her.

Chapter three

Quasi-corporeal companions in popular culture

It is a never-ending source of fascination to me that the phenomenon of quasi-corporeal companions stubbornly refuses to create a niche for itself in the mainstream of paranormal literature and research. My experience has led me to conclude that more people 'see' QCCs than see ghosts or UFOs, and yet the subject is rarely if ever covered in journals and newsletters that most paranormalists read avidly.

Nevertheless, QCCs occasionally find their way into the public eye. In 1991, the film *Drop Dead Fred*, starring Rik Mayall, was generally well-received although it was given 'mixed reviews', as they say in Hollywood.

In the film, a young woman who's trying to 'find herself' ends up in a battle royal with her domineering mother. Simultaneously saddled with a philandering spouse and devastated at the loss of her purse, automobile and employment, she seeks solace from her newly-returned quasi-corporeal companion, Fred.

The following April, *Star Trek: The Next Generation* got in on the act with a well-crafted episode entitled *Imaginary Friend*. In the programme, little Clara has an 'imaginary' companion aboard the *Enterprise* who initially seems all 'sweetness and light' but Isabella quickly demonstrates that she has a dark side. In fact, the safety of the entire *Enterprise* crew is threatened.

Although Isabella's true nature is eventually discovered – she's an alien who sneaks on board while the starship is exploring a nebula that's formed around a neutron star – we can forgive the scriptwriters for coming up with an explanation that is almost certainly not correct in real life. After all, *Star Trek* is science fiction. In fact, the episode is hugely enjoyable and, if nothing else, at least draws attention to the phenomenon, if not explaining it.

Over the years, the QCC phenomenon has been used light-heartedly in TV ads to sell everything from household cleaners to beefburgers. And yet, if you were to ask a random selection of people in a busy street if they remember the above examples, few if any will. I know, because I've done just that. I asked one hundred adults if they could name any fictional or non-fictional TV programme, advert or movie that dealt with the subject of 'imaginary childhood friends'. Three mentioned *Drop Dead Fred*; the rest were unable to recall anything at all.

Moving out of the realms of science fiction and comedy, there is one notable incident in modern history which has a QCC angle to it. Unfortunately it is deeply unpleasant.

Kurt Cobain was the lead singer, guitarist and songwriter with the legendary rock band Nirvana. More than that, he was viewed by many as the 'spiritual leader' of the band, as if Nirvana's very essence was encapsulated in the man. Cobain became a world-famous celebrity. Songs such as *Smells Like Teen Spirit* and *Heart-Shaped Box* were adopted as anthems by teenagers all over the world. The problem was that Cobain never wanted to become a celebrity, but found to his dissatisfaction that fame and fronting up a rock band are not easily separated.

Kurt Cobain left a drug rehabilitation centre in Marina Del Rey, California, on 1 April, 1994. Later, he was reported missing. Within the space of one week he was found dead, having apparently committed suicide. I say 'apparently' because rumours have persisted that Cobain did not take his own life, and that he was in fact murdered.

A note was found beside his body which, despite a paucity of convincing evidence, was soon labelled as a suicide note. Regardless, this sad epistle makes interesting reading.

> To Boddah pronounced,
>
> Speaking from the tongue of an experienced simpleton who obviously would rather be an emasculated, infantile complainee, this note should be pretty easy to understand.
>
> All the warnings from the punk rock 101 courses over the years, since my first introduction to the, shall we say, ethic involved with independence and the embracement of your community has proven to be very

true. I haven't felt the excitement of listening to as well as creating music along with reading and writing for to many years now. I feel guilty beyond words about these things.

For example, when we're back stage and the lights go out and the manic roar of the crowds begin, OT doesn't affect me the way in which it did for Freddie Mercury, who seemed to love, relish in the love and adoration from the crowd which is something I totally admire and envy. The fact is, I can't fool you, any one of you. It simply isn't fair to you or me. The worst crime I can think of would be to rip people off by faking it and pretending as if I'm having 100% fun.

Sometimes I feel as if I should have a punch-in time clock before I walk out on stage. I've tried everything within my power to appreciate it (and I do, God believe me I do, but its not enough). I appreciate the fact that I and we have affected and entertained a lot of people. It must be one of those narcissists who only appreciate things when they're gone. I'm too sensitive. I need to be slightly numb in order to regain the enthusiasms I once had as a child.

On our last 3 tours, I've had a much better appreciation for all the people I've known personally, and as fans of our music, but I still can't get over the frustration, the guilt and empathy I have for everyone. There's good in all of us and I think I simply love people too much, so much that it makes me feel to sad. The sad little, sensitive, unappreciative, Pisces, Jesus man. Why don't you just enjoy it? I don't know!!

I don't have a goddess of a wife who sweats ambition and empathy and a daughter who reminds me too much of what I used to be, full of love and joy, kissing every person she meets because everyone is good and will do her no harm. And that terrifies me to the point to where I can barely function. I can't stand the thought of Frances becoming the miserable, self-destructive, death rocker that I've become.

I have it good, very good, and I'm grateful, but since the age of seven, I've become hateful towards all humans in general. Only because it seems so easy for people to get along that have empathy. Only because I love and feel sorry for people too much, I guess.

Thank you all from the pit of my burning, nauseous stomach for your letters and concern during the past years. I'm too much of an erratic moody baby! I don't have the passion anymore, so remember, It's better to burn out then to fade away.

Peace, love, empathy,
Kurt Cobain

The note had a postscript which read, 'Frances and Courtney, I'll be at your alter. Please keep going Courtney for Frances for her life which will be so much happier without me. I Love you. I love you! '

Doubt has been cast as to whether Cobain penned this last sentence, in which he refers to his then partner Courtney Love and daughter Frances, but it is not within the scope of this book to determine either the nature of Cobain's death or the authenticity of the last part of the 'suicide note' left behind. The official verdict *is* suicide, and unless powerful evidence to the contrary emerges then I think we should accept it. To cry, 'Murder most foul!' when no murder may have been committed is a risky business, and will inevitably lead to the pointing of fingers at people who may well be innocent.

What *is* obvious is that Cobain was a deeply troubled young man. Less obvious, even to his fans, is the identity of the 'Boddah' to whom the letter is addressed.

Curt Cobain had an interest in Buddhism. After he died he was cremated, with one-third of his ashes scattered at the Namgyal Tibetan Buddhist Monastery in Ithaca, New York. This has led some to suggest that 'Boddah' should actually read 'Buddha'. For a number of reasons I must take issue with notion.

Firstly, despite the fact that Cobain was a good lyricist he was not the most skilled of writers. Writing the words to a rock song cannot be compared to penning an op-ed column for the Washington Post. Nevertheless, Cobain was far from illiterate. His spelling isn't brilliant, but neither is it atrocious. It seems ludicrous to me that someone of Cobain's intelligence would have mis-spelt 'Buddha' as 'Boddah'.

Further, a cursory examination of the note gives us some pointers as to just who Boddah is, and it certainly isn't the holy man who gained enlightenment sitting under a fig tree.

Early in the note Cobain states, '...since my first introduction to the, shall we say, ethic involved with independence and the embracement of your community...' It is clear from this that 'Boddah' is not on his own. He belongs to a 'community' or group of people towards which Cobain has positive feelings. In fact, 'Boddah' was a quasi-corporeal companion that entertained Cobain at various junctures during his childhood. Initially, Cobain had called him 'Bodah', the second letter 'd' being added to his name later. From the contents of the note the singer left behind, it is clear that Boddah, who had been with Cobain since he was a youngster, accompanied him almost literally to the grave.

The QCC phenomenon is almost like the fortean equivalent of the emperor's new clothes. There is a problem, but it is rarely discussed. This is unfortunate, for it is a phenomenon that is one of the truly uncharted territories of paranormal research.

Chapter four

The times they are fortean...

On 2 January, 2006, I received an email from a *Bizarre* reader called John Garrick. He related to me his QCC experience, and just over two weeks later, his story appeared in print.

Many years ago, John lived in Jarrow, a town at the centre of the north-east's industrial heartland. Coincidentally, I spent much of my youth living in Jarrow, although my quasi-corporeal companions had long-since faded into memory.

John's memories of his family home are a little vague, as he was only six at the time. However, he vividly recollects his young playmate, Victoria.

> Victoria was really funny. She was two years older than me, and really mischievous. One day, when we were playing in the back yard, she made me pile up lots of bricks in front of the yard door. I remember laughing hysterically when my Dad was pushing against it from the outside and wondering why it wouldn't open.

Victoria was, according to John, a normal child in just about every way. Every way but one, that is, for the only person who could actually see Victoria was John himself.

Some researchers have suggested that up to one-third of children have had what are commonly called 'imaginary childhood friends'. Conventional wisdom suggests that these companions are merely imaginary companions dreamed up by lonely children who don't see enough of their more corporeal chums. I don't believe this to be true, for reasons which will become clear later in this volume.

Another reader contacted me in response to John's story, and related her own experience. Her QCC was called Edward:

> Edward always used to wear these checked suits that looked very Edwardian. He was very serious and never

seemed to want to play games. He just wanted to talk all the time.

I remember sitting on the sofa with him. He would fold his hands in his lap and start talking about nature, science, history....he was a regular brain-box.

One day my mother found an old, wooden nib-pen on the sofa where he'd been sitting. She kept asking me where it had come from.

I wanted to tell her it was Edward's, but I couldn't because I knew she'd get angry. I'd told her about Edward before, and she just kept telling me he didn't exist and I was to stop being silly.

After she found the pen she kept looking at me in an odd way. It was as if she sensed I knew something. She threw the pen on the fire and told me not to say anything to my father.

These two experiences with QCCs reinforced my belief that the phenomenon, whatever its nature, was not imaginary. I became convinced that quasi-corporeal companions have an objective reality of some kind, but one which is not well understood.

Another reader sent me a letter via the *Shields Gazette's* office in South Shields, and related his own QCC story. Graham Smith is a computer technician who now lives and works in Spain. His father was an army officer, and as a child Graham became used to moving around the country. At the age of seven, the Smith family relocated to the midlands and stayed there for three years. It was there that Graham had his first QCC experience.

My mother used to look after two local children whose parents both worked. Their father used to pay her a few pounds for this. She didn't really need the money, but it kept her busy and she was one of these women who loved having kids around all the time.

I don't remember much about the children she looked after, except that they were two boys, and their names were Kevin and Tony. One day, their parents dropped off Kevin on his own as they had to take Tony to the hospital. There was another boy in our house at the same time, called Michael. I didn't know where he came from, but we played all day.

Eventually, Kevin's parents came to collect him. They were very upset, and I found out later that Tony had died. I don't know what the cause was, but my mother said that there had been 'something wrong with his blood', so it might have been leukaemia. I remember that Michael went away at around the same time, although he did come back later the next day.

I told my mother about the 'strange boy' who had been playing with us, and she got upset. Later, I heard her telling my father that it might have been 'Tony's ghost', but I know it wasn't. He was definitely called Michael, and he looked nothing like Tony.

Michael used to come to our house a lot to play, but no one else ever seemed to see him. On the day Tony died, Kevin never saw him either; or at least, I don't remember Kevin ever speaking to Michael.

I told my grandmother about Michael, and she asked me where he came from. I didn't know, but the next time he came to see me I asked him. He just said, 'From the funny place', and left it at that.

After we relocated to Newcastle, I never saw Michael again.

There are two interesting aspects to Graham's story. Firstly, Michael would not (or perhaps could not) divulge exactly where he came from. Secondly, when the Smith family moved to Newcastle upon Tyne, Michael seemingly stayed put and Graham never saw him again. As I researched the QCC phenomenon, it became clear to me that these two factors were common denominators scattered throughout the field. QCCs never seemed to divulge exactly where they came from, and they never moved house along with their fully-corporeal companion. This intrigued me, and I wanted to know why.

Shortly before my second article on the QCC phenomenon appeared in the *Shields Gazette*, I penned a letter to the *Fortean Times*. It was published in the February 2006 issue. I told readers that I believed the phenomenon was not purely imaginary, and that I intended to write a book on the subject:

I'm currently compiling a book on the subjec
'imaginary' childhood friends. Some research
suggested that up to 30 per cent of youngster
have had an 'imaginary' friend during their fc
years; a friend whom they played with, talke
interacted with in other ways, but who, notably, was
entirely invisible to others.

I had two such friends around the age of five, and I'm
far from convinced that such companions are imaginary
at all, and may actually enjoy some form of objective
existence that is little understood.

I would be interested in hearing from FT readers who
had such childhood companions and who would
consider allowing me to relate their experiences.

I was staggered at the response, and received emails from numerous
countries, including India, Holland and the USA. Many of the tales
related to me by QCC experients have been included in this volume.

Up to this juncture, my picture of the QCC phenomenon had been
quite simplistic. I believed that quasi-corporeal companions were,
essentially, invisible kids who were relatively normal other than their
ability to appear and disappear at will. As an experienced paranormal
investigator, I should have known better. Fortean phenomena are
never simple. Just as you think you've got a handle on a mystery, you
can bet your boots that some data will present itself to skew the pot
and make you rethink everything you know.

Slowly but surely, I came to see that there were several distinct kinds
of QCC. By far the most populous type comprised the 'imaginary
friends' who, apart from their spontaneous arrivals and departures,
behaved entirely as one expects 'normal' children to. But there were
other types. Superficially they seemed to have little in common with
the more conventional 'invisible kids', but there were curious parallels
that led me to think there was a connection. The more I studied the
phenomenon, the more obvious those parallels became.

Chapter five

Boring old Andrina

Writer Lynn C. Doyle – don't you just love that pen name – is 41 and, in the realms of QCC research, quite a rare commodity. Despite the fact that she crossed over the threshold of puberty some considerable time ago, she still has regular contact with a number of her quasi-corporeal pals. Far from finding this in any way disturbing – or at the very least a considerable distraction – Lynn is able to see the funny side and write about it with a degree of irony and wit.

> I still have several friends without a form. In fact, one of them turned up on the last census. If accused, my husband was going to get a philosophy professor from the University of Essex to argue that existence isn't predicated on a corporeal entity.

Before we look at Lynn's QCC entourage a little more closely we need to examine her childhood circumstances, for it is on the basis of these circumstances that Lynn has formulated a clear perception of both the nature and origin of QCCs, or at least her very own quasi-corporeal companions. Her arguments cannot be dismissed lightly.

> I was effectively an only child, as there was a large gap between my older siblings and I. I spent large amounts of my childhood being utterly bored. Sometimes I would pretend that I was adopted and that my real parents were gypsies, or in the circus or something. I also used to play with names a lot. I grew up in Ireland, but because I used to read English comics and the works of Enid Blyton, the names I gave my pretend people were a real cultural mishmash. I think this was compounded by the fact that some of the stories in the comics were about people from 'other' cultures, so my characters could easily be Sino/British/Irish/Turkish, and never seemed in the least odd.

Quite clearly, from Lynn's perspective, she was responsible for creating her own QCCs and also for naming them. She also seems to believe that their *raison d'etre* was to cure her boredom. Enjoying a level of interaction with her siblings that was insufficient to entertain her, she seemingly invented a number of imaginary friends to fill the gap.

Lynn has also offered up an explanation for the bizarre nomenclature which, as we shall see, often infects the world of the QCC. In my research I have stumbled across QCCs called Forkkstabb, Beevonga, Kreb-Ash, Vertical Upwards and Soggybox. A name given to a quasi-corporeal friend may be, to use Lynn's wordage, a 'mishmash' created from two or more cultural settings. If Lynn is correct, then we may have the first glimmers of an explanation for other strangely-named QCCs. The question that must first be asked, however, is whether Lynn's explanations holds good in some or all cases, or perhaps none at all.

From a purely logical perspective, the idea of a bored child inventing imaginary companions for social and mental stimulation makes good sense. Further, it surely cannot be denied that – perhaps in many cases, who knows – QCCs are just that; imaginary friends conjured up by the experients to fill a temporary but real vacuum in their lives. Even if there is ultimately no proof that QCCs are created in, and eventually emerge from, the subconscious, we still cannot deny the possibility. Absence of evidence, we know, is not evidence of absence. Whether all QCCs can be explained in like manner is something that we will discuss presently. For now, however, we will return to Lynn and her quasi-corporeal playmates.

> From childhood, there was a little girl who did all the
> naughty things I didn't want to cop the blame for.
> Anyway, my childhood friend was called 'Andrina'. I
> don't remember much about her, except, as I said, that
> she was supposed to cop the blame for the things I did
> that weren't considered desirable.

Inventing a fictitious personage to shoulder the blame for our childhood indiscretions also makes sense. If we can offload onto Andrina and her quasi-corporeal colleagues the responsibility for our naughtiness, then we can side-step both blame and punishment in one fell swoop. Interestingly, though, this was not a common theme unearthed during my research. Many experients admitted inventing imaginary children to take the blame for their own actions, but few of these imaginary characters if any could be classed as quasi-corporeal entities in any meaningful sense.

Geoff Barnstead told me that he would sometimes blame his own misbehaviour on an imaginary 'someone else', but the person he invented to take the blame would only 'exist' until the heat was off, so to speak, and the threat of parental punishment had passed. The personages expediently invented to take the blame for wrongdoing are normally short-lived, almost totally devoid of character and personality and, if they have a physical description, it is offered by the experient only to make their invention more believable to others.

By way of example, Geoff remembers once hitting a drainpipe with a lump of wood outside of his grandmother's house. The drainpipe cracked and Geoff panicked. He subsequently claimed that a 'big boy with blond hair and a white jumper with a red, zigzag hoop on it' had walked into the garden, threatened him and then whacked the drainpipe with the wooden stave before running off. Geoff thinks that both his grandmother and parents were suspicious of his story and thereafter harboured serious doubts about his innocence. They couldn't prove he was lying, however, and guardedly gave him the benefit of the doubt. Geoff's ploy had worked. His relatively detailed description of the alleged assailant served no purpose other than to make his story sound convincing. It did, and he escaped punishment. Once the mystery aggressor had served his purpose he was resigned to oblivion, brutally despatched back to the eternal state of non-existence that he never really escaped from in the first place.

The interesting thing is that Geoff had two long-time QCCs – Brian and Nicola – that he could easily have blamed for cracking his grandmother's drainpipe had he wished. I asked him why he hadn't blamed them instead of inventing someone from scratch. His answer was telling. He looked at me with astonishment, as if the answer to the question was so apparent that the very asking of it was an affront. 'But they didn't *do* it! How would *you* like to be blamed for something you hadn't done?'

As a child Geoff had been prepared to compromise his principles to the extent of diverting blame away from himself, but he would never have gone so far as to blame another person for his own actions; that would be a stretch too far. The boy that Geoff blamed for the damage was entirely fictitious and would never suffer as a result of Geoff's lies. He could never be caught, never be punished. He would never cry tears of bitterness as a result of being wrongly accused and blamed for something he'd never done. This knowledge assuaged Geoff's conscience. However, because Brian and Nicola were real to Geoff, the idea of blaming them for the damage was unthinkable. They were his friends, and much as Geoff wanted to avoid being punished he would never stoop so low as to blame two good pals for his own actions.

During my research I found this to be a consistent pattern. Experients would sometimes invent imaginary characters for their own ends, but these were never confused with their QCCs. To the experients, the difference between the transient, imaginary characters invented for expediency and true QCCs was enormous.

Tracy Gourley from Boise, Idaho had a QCC called Jodie, although she sometimes went by the nick-name Jo-Jo.

Sometimes, Tracy would want to go out with friends but was worried that her mother would not allow her to. Consequently she invented an imaginary classmate called Letisha. Whenever she wanted to go out with her friends she would simply tell her mother that she was 'going to Letisha's house to study'. I asked Tracy why she didn't just say that she was at Jodie's. 'How could I do that? That's ridiculous! Jodie lived here... in *my* house! Anyway, I don't think Jodie would have liked it if I'd lied to Mom, particularly if I'd dragged her into the lie.'

In the case of Andrina there exists a doubt as to whether she is merely a character of expedience, a true QCC or, confusingly, something in between. Nothing, I have found in the parallel universe inhabited by our quasi-corporeal friends is easy to figure out.

Andrina's character was hardly scintillating. She seems to have been rather one-dimensional and Lynn herself admits that she doesn't remember much about her. This doesn't exactly sit well with Lynn 's belief that she may have invented Andrina as a substitute for interacting with her siblings. If one was to invent a playmate, wouldn't it be logical to invent one who had some verve? Further, Lynn herself offers the alternative explanation that Andrina was invented to take the blame when she was naughty. Lynn's integrity as she relates her account is beyond question. She recalls her interaction with quasi-corporeal friends without any exaggeration but with a great deal of self-deprecating humour. I am sure that when she tries to explain or rationalise her QCC experiences she is being impeccably genuine, but if she can offer two alternative explanations for her experiences is it possible that, deep down, she may not be entirely sure herself?

Lynn takes up the story:

> Far more interesting, I think, are the worlds I used to
> invent. I came to England to study in the 80s, and a
> whole new generation of imaginaries grew up. Although
> basically childish and anarchic, I was old enough by
> then to fit them into stories/worlds that made a kind of
> external sense.

And at this juncture it may be worth remembering that Lynn's
childhood was spent in Ireland where belief in other worlds or
dimensions beyond the normal senses is well accepted by the general
populace. Lynn is also a writer who, like most pensmiths, possesses
creativity in extra abundance. Culturally and professionally, then, Lynn
C. Doyle has the right tools to create 'imaginary' friends; or, just
possibly, the right tools to visualise something that is already there.

Lynn herself admits that creativity and imagination probably play a
part in the emergence of her QCCs from wherever they come from:
'Personally I think it's just story-telling writ large, though I appreciate
that the infirm-of-mind could get confused between alternative
realities.'

Perhaps. Or, just maybe, we of sound mind sometimes get confused by
external realities that haven't previously figured in our view of this
exceedingly complex universe.

Chapter six

Type 1: the Invizikids

By far the most common type of QCC is the 'Invizikid'. I coined this colloquialism as a title for a lecture I once delivered on the subject, and it stuck. It may not have the lofty ring of scientific nomenclature, but the fact is that I don't pretend to be a scientist. I've already spelt out my reasons for not feeling comfortable with the use of the word 'invisible' on a technical level, but the epithet Invizikid rolls nicely off the tongue, so – logic aside – I'll stick with it.

As previously described, Invizikids bear a strong resemblance to ordinary children. They look completely conventional, dress in a conventional manner which is usually in keeping with their cultural surroundings and time setting, and act exactly as we would expect children to act.

In my research, I found that around seventy percent of experients described their QCCs with conventional names. These names were also culturally, sexually and linguistically correct. English Invizikids would have English names, for example. Females would be called Elizabeth, Erica or Julie, while males would be called John, Norman or Peter, and so on. French Invizikids had French names, Portuguese Invizikids had Portuguese names, and Chinese Invizikids had Chinese names. The use of proper names, in these cases, simply served to reinforce the 'normal' appearance and aura of this type of QCC.

Around thirty percent of the time, the QCCs of Type 1 would not have conventional names. Instead, they would bear titles such as Won-Won, Rallie-Rallie or Waffa-Waffa. This curious use of names which we may call 'double-barrelled repetitives' is something which cuts right across geographical, spiritual, religious and cultural boundaries when one is examining the QCC experience. Why this is so is a mystery, and to date I can find no logical reason for it. Nevertheless, the observation is useful because it helps us understand that the appearance of quasi-corporeal companions is a trans-global phenomenon with peculiar but consistent characteristics.

nvizikids are almost always good-natured. They can get a little cranky or bad-tempered from time-to-time, occasionally displaying fits of petulance if they don't get their own way, but I have only once come across an Invizikid who was violent or flew into a rage.

Invizikids will play games and engage in other activities with experients, including sporting activities and indoor games. They will play with toys, and on occasion even help experients 'tidy-up' afterwards.

When Invizikids do their disappearing act, it will normally take one of two forms. Some Type 1 QCCs will remain visible to the experient when another person enters the room. While they are present the experient may see them while others cannot. This implies that their ability to become invisible is selective. Others will always become invisible to the experient too, suggesting that while some QCCs can choose who they become invisible to at any given time, others only have the ability to be either visible or invisible to everyone at once.

Whenever experients question their Type 1 QCC about their origins, such as asking them where they live, or where they come from, the QCC will almost always be vague when answering. Typically they'll respond, 'From far away', or 'From another place'. Curiously, they may occasionally claim to live on a vehicle which is always on the move, which makes it difficult to ascertain where they hail from. The mother of one youngster told me that his Type 1 QCC 'lived on a big red bus'.

During 2006, my colleague Darren Ritson – a paranormal investigator from North Tyneside – and I spent several months investigating a protracted and extremely intense poltergeist case. There also happened to be a young child living in the house who had a QCC called Sammy. I interviewed the child about his allegedly imaginary friend, and he openly admitted that 'Sammy' often talked to him. However, whenever I asked him exactly what Sammy said to him, he'd go all coy and simply respond, 'I don't know'. This, I found, was another common denominator with Type 1 QCCs; experients will readily admit that their quasi-corporeal companions engage them in conversation, but they will often refuse to repeat anything they actually say. When the young experient in question was pushed on this point, he would only say, 'It's a secret'. Like the use of the 'double-barrelled repetitive', this feature in Type 1 cases is something of a mystery.

Chapter seven

Alan Donnelly and the heretical Mr Gubby

The sharing of the same QCC by two experients is rare, but not unknown as I shall demonstrate in a later chapter. Far more common is the scenario in which two siblings have their own 'QCC experience' simultaneously, again adding doubt to the idea that QCCs are simply invented by lonely children without company.

Alan Donnelly had a QCC at the age of four or thereabouts, as did his sister. His interpretation of the nature of QCCs, half a century after the event, is interesting.

> I am curious to know in what way such things could
> normally be considered to have an objective existence,
> other than by people who adhere to either a
> pagan/magical belief system or conceivably to the
> heretical Christian 'word of faith' scam...

This is an interesting approach. Alan seems to be suggesting that experients may judge the potential objective existence of QCCs not on the weight of the evidence, but rather on the basis of one's own belief system. In other words, QCCs may be real to *me* not primarily because witnesses claim to see them, but simply because my belief system allows me to more easily incorporate QCCs into my world-view. I think there is a large degree of truth in this. The vast majority of evangelical Christians I interviewed believed that QCCs were either entirely imaginary or – a far more sinister interpretation – evil spirits trying to delude the experients away from the Christian path. Conversely, almost all Druids, Wiccans and pagans of other persuasions were quite comfortable with the idea that QCCs were some sort of discarnate spirit or sentient elemental energy.

Alan went on to relate to me his own experience: 'For what it's worth, my friend was a Mr Gubby – and half a century or so on I really can't remember how I envisaged him.'

This was another factor that I found to be extremely common with experients. Many had vivid memories of having a QCC as a child, but those who interacted with Type 2 and Type 3 QCCs often lost their ability to recall what they looked like in later life. Intriguingly, they could readily articulate *what* their QCC was, but struggled to describe its exact appearance.

One experient, Margaret Braun of Berlin, had a weasel (called Agrarus) as a QCC, but told me that she could not visualise him in her mind. Not only could she not 'see' Agrarus as he appeared to her as a child, but she could not picture a weasel of any description when she tried to recall her childhood companion.

> It is like.... when I think of Agrarus my brain won't let me think of a weasel at the same time, you know? I can picture a weasel – any weasel – in my head, but as soon as I think of Agrarus the picture of the weasel disappears. It is so weird. Sometimes I think that Agrarus is still around... I think he stops me from seeing him or remembering him like he was. He just won't let my brain remember what he looked like. Why would he do that?

Why indeed? Now back to Alan Donnelly and Mr Gubby.

'I think that I didn't have any clear idea at all of how he may have looked or sounded.' said Alan, but the fact is that he must have had at the time for otherwise he simply wouldn't have been able to interact with Mr Gubby in any meaningful way. It is almost certain that Alan could at one time 'see' and 'hear' Mr Gubby in a real sense, but that later he simply lost the ability to recall these incidents. This inability to recall anything visually or aurally about their QCC post-experience is extremely common.

Alan went on to describe his sister's QCC:

> However, I know my sister's imaginary friend did have an objective reality; I think he was befriended because of the sonorous nature of his name: Mr Selwyn Lloyd. (If you are of a generation which doesn't recognise the name, then try Googling it!)

Baron John Selwyn Lloyd was, of course, the Tory Chancellor of the Exchequer between 1960 and 1962, and also Speaker of the House of Commons. He is best remembered for his creation of the National Economic Development Council. He was an able enough politician, but became unpopular when he introduced a policy of wage restraint in an effort to cure rising inflation. The move wasn't popular with the trade unions, and he was eventually left with no real option but to resign.

Alan Donnelly is correct to describe the name of Selwyn Lloyd as sonorous, but although he was underestimated as a politician there were other more likely candidates in the political arena at that time if one were seeking a role model. Why this QCC should call himself Selwyn Lloyd, then, is a mystery, unless the epithet was simply foisted upon him by Alan's sister after she randomly plucked it out of the air.

Like her brother's friend Mr Gubby, Selwyn Lloyd seems to have gone into retirement; perhaps enjoying life in the netherworld's equivalent of a rest home. Whatever, I wish them well.

Chapter eight

Quasi-corporeal number crunching

Research carried out in the USA by psychologists from the University of Washington and the University of Oregon* has shown that, by the age of seven, over two-thirds of children have had a QCC experience of some kind. If the phenomenon is not purely psychological, and truly does have some paranormal aspect to it, then the conclusions we can draw are simply breathtaking. Imagine what the reaction in the media would be if two well-respected schools of learning suddenly validated the alien abduction theory, and, further, suggested that two-thirds of our youngsters may have been temporarily kidnapped by visitors from outer space!

Of course, psychologists are almost guaranteed to reject any consideration of paranormality when it comes to the NCC phenomenon. However, commonly-held notions about it are now being treated with a growing degree of suspicion.

One popular idea, discussed earlier, is that 'imaginary' childhood friends are conjured up by lonely children. Ask just about anyone who has ever heard of the phenomenon what precipitates it, and you will likely receive one of two stock answers. Most psychologists argue that youngsters create imaginary friends when they are short of siblings to interact with. If you ain't got a brother, make one. Short of a sister? Build one in your head.

Of course, this may well hold true in some cases, but my research has shown me that the majority of 'imaginary' friends actually belong to children who already have siblings, and it is at this juncture that the second explanation usually raises its head.

---

*   Taylor, M., *et al*. 2004. 'The characteristics and correlates of fantasy in school-age children: Imaginary companions, impersonation, and social understanding.' *Developmental Psychology* 40 (November): 1173–87.

'Ah', say the psycho-sages, 'When there are brothers and sisters at home taking all the attention, then kids will invent an imaginary playmate that they can "keep to themselves" and don't have to share.'

So they you have it. Kids with allegedly imaginary friends invent them either because they have no siblings or because they do have them. This is an argument which, I would venture, pretty much sows up all the possibilities; but it is flawed. Why? Quite simply, because you can't have your cake and eat it. Conventional explanations for the QCC phenomenon are built upon the premise that 'imaginary' childhood friends really are imaginary, and arrogantly ignore many other potential explanations.

Research has also shown that QCCs are as common among those in primary school as they are with those of pre-school age. If the theory that QCCs were created by lonely children was true, then one would imagine a significant number of experients among the pre-school age group – followed by a sharp decline when they began to attend nursery or school or kindergarten, where they would no longer be lonely. In fact, the statistics give the lie to this idea completely; a *greater* percentage of school-age kids have QCCs than pre-school children!

Generally speaking, most QCC experients have one 'companion' at a time. In my own experience, my two companions never appeared together, and the appearance of one for the first time only followed the disappearance of the other for the last time. Serial experients – that is, those who have a succession of QCCs, one after the other – are not uncommon. However, simultaneous QCC experients – those who have more than one QCC at the same time – are rarer. There is some, slight evidence that simultaneous experients are more common in the USA than elsewhere, but it may be dangerous to read too much into this.

Simultaneous experients, I have found, rarely have more than two QCCs. I once interviewed someone who claimed to have had four QCCs simultaneously, and in the USA one experient apparently reported having thirteen.

Research has also shown that children who experience the QCC phenomenon do not always see the Type 1 QCC exclusively. Some have QCCs that are likened to dolls, stuffed toys, items of furniture and animals.

Early-age experients – of pre-school age – are more likely to be girls. However, among older experients the proportions balance out and just as many males have QCCs as females. In the USA, I found that just over half of QCCs are Type 1, whereas in my research the number elsewhere was greater – around seventy percent.

In the final analysis, the relevance of statistics depends on the mind-set of the investigator. To some they will be of crucial importance, while to others they will be little short of meaningless. Personally, I like to savour paranormal phenomena instead of clinically dissecting them. For this reason I have included relatively little in the way of statistics in this book. My own feeling is that an obsession with statistics rarely leads to any great understanding in the field of paranormal research. The UFO phenomenon is, perhaps, the greatest example. For decades, investigators have tried to understand the phenomenon by number-crunching, and the results have been woefully inadequate. Some like to scrutinise the recipe, whereas I prefer to eat the cake.

Chapter nine

Carol, Fred and the Binks factor

Carol M. responded to my request in the *Fortean Times* for QCC experiences, and told me of her own when she was just five years old. Carol's friend was a Type 4 QCC – more about this later – and lived in the wardrobe situated in her bedroom. He was a Native American and called, somewhat incongruously, 'Fred'.

During my research into this book I noticed that the names given to (or by) QCCs were often disassociated culturally from their apparent background. Chinese doctors would be called Ian, Buddhist monks would be named Brian and ancient Sumerian warlords could easily carry the illustrious epithet Kevin or Norman. One correspondent, Cherie Dalton, had a QCC called Wilma. Wilma was a Japanese mermaid who had, if we believe her story, died in the mid-fifteenth century.

I dare say that, to some researchers, this culturally fractured form of nomenclature would be evidence that the QCCs can have no basis in reality. I'm not so sure. The very oddness of these names hints to me that the phenomenon is a genuine one. If someone was to invent a Native American QCC, Running Bear or Crazy Deer would be more logical choices if we wanted to create a more authentic character. Of course, it could be argued that QCC experients are generally so young that their awareness of cultural propriety hasn't had time to develop. To a six-year-old, Jeremy may seem as fitting a name for an ancient Viking as Olaf or Harald. The problem is that these incongruities show no signs of diminishing even when the experients are aged nine, ten or older. Also, QCCs of a seemingly British-European origin, whom one would often expect to have regular names such as Joe, Jill or Dianne, may sometimes have bizarre names like Gooty, Frab-Frab or Graloona. It is well within the cultural grasp of a nine-year-old to recognise that Frab-Frab is not a 'normal' name, and yet Frab-Frab it will be as opposed to Frances, Hannah or Julie.

It is difficult to give a sensible explanation for this aspect of the QCC phenomenon. Do QCCs live in a world or dimension where the normal rules and conventions surrounding nomenclature do not apply? Or could it be that, at least on some occasions, the name is given to the QCC by the experient and the QCC is quite happy to accept it? I honestly do not know, although further research may well shed some light on the matter.

But I digress. At this juncture I think we should return to Fred in the wardrobe. Carol herself admits that Fred may have in some sense been her own creation.

> I think he was around when I was four or five, in the
> late Sixties, and I'm sure he was inspired by a picture of
> someone in a war bonnet in a book at school.

Intriguingly, Fred usually appeared to Carol in a war bonnet made from eagle feathers.

Of course, even if Fred was in some way 'brought into existence' by Carol it does not mean that he isn't real. There is a hallowed tradition in some cultures of creating 'thought-forms' like the Tibetan *tulpas*, and we cannot deny the possibility that, at least in some cases, this is exactly what QCCs are.

Carol seems to be aware of one of the more common explanations for QCCs, namely, that they are imaginary playmates created by children who are feeling lonely or in some way socially disenfranchised. 'I had a baby sister at the time, so no doubt I was feeling a bit ignored and wanted the company,' Carol told me.

I have problems with this idea, as the reader will have by now gathered. Researchers can't have it both ways. If QCCs are there to fill the gap when we don't have a sibling to play with – or alternatively give us someone to keep us company when a new sibling arrives – then we should *all* have QCCs whether we are an only child or, conversely, living in a house filled with boisterous brothers and sisters. My own feeling is that the presence or absence of siblings is largely irrelevant when trying to assess reasons for the presence of a QCC in the life of a child.

Carol eventually lost touch with Fred. 'I can't remember when he left, and I'm afraid I've got no real memories of us doing stuff together or any history I might have invented for him.'

Then, on reflection, she did recall something:

> I've remembered something that my Mum told me I used to do when I was very small, about 2 or 3, before Fred turned up.
>
> I used to pick up small, invisible things from the carpet with my thumb and first finger and offer them to people saying, 'Want a bink?'
>
> Taid [Welsh for Grandad] used to find it hugely amusing. I haven't got the faintest idea what 'binks' were or what they might have looked like – were they some sort of a precursor to Fred, or something completely different?

I did a search on the Internet to try and establish just what a 'bink' may have been. Short of stumbling across a character from *Star Wars* called Jar Jar Binks, I didn't come up with much, and as Carol's experience took place before Jar Jar Binks had been invented it's difficult to foist any importance on the similarity.

Carol wanted to know if other correspondents had reported similar experiences. None reported having a QCC quite like Fred the Indian or finding a handy supply of binks on the living room carpet, but that's QCCs for you. Every one I've ever investigated has a set of unique features not found in any others.

Carol emailed me again and told me that she had a friend who had an 'imaginary' companion as a child. 'It was an 'imaginary' horse called Pebbles, which I think is rather cool. I suspect imaginary animals are a bit more unusual than imaginary people, especially animals as big as horses.' The truth is that animal QCCs are quite common, as we shall see, and they come in a wonderful variety of shapes and sizes.

Chapter ten

Type 2: the Elementals

Belief in 'elemental' spirits has a long and hallowed tradition in the British Isles. For readers who are not conversant with the idea, a word of explanation may be appropriate at this juncture.

Nature-based spiritual belief systems, usually practised most vigorously by indigenous peoples across the globe, often teach that the universe as we know it is composed of four 'elements' or 'principles'. Traditionally, these are *fire, water, earth* and *air*. There has long been a belief that each of these elements has a particular type of 'spirit' attached to it; not just an essence or characteristic, but often a sentient creature or group of creatures who seemingly have an affinity with the element in question.

The concept of 'elemental spirits' probably arose at the dawn of human history, and is certainly not new. However, credit for codifying the concept and providing it with a coherent framework is usually given to the Swiss physician and alchemist, Paracelsus. Paracelsus was born on November 10, 1493, in Einsiedeln, Switzerland. He grew to become a doctor of some renown, and favoured the use of mineral-based treatments for disease at the expense of organic or herbal counterparts. Paracelsus was also a devout occultist, and was fascinated with 'the elements' and the spirit creatures which may, albeit invisibly, be attached to them.

Paracelsus taught that the elements had a natural way of balancing each other. Water could quench fire, for instance, but fire could also evaporate water. The earth could 'capture' or 'hold' air, but the air (read, 'wind') could also disperse the earth. And so on and so forth. Of course, having attributed *intent* to the actions of the elements, it was only a small step forward to attach intelligence to them.

According to Paracelsus, the elemental of the Fire Element was the salamander. Actually, it was the good doctor himself who thought up this association. Never before had the humble salamander been connected alchemically or in any other way with so much as a box of matches, but the idea quickly took hold.

Before too long, the word *salamander* was being used to describe just about anything that had a vague connection with fire or heat. Pokers were called salamanders, as were small ovens. The nuggets of slag left over in blast furnaces were referred to as salamanders, too, and chefs even started to call the caramelising tools used in their kitchens... erm, *salamanders.*

The water elementals were called by Paracelsus *Undines*, named after the water nymph Ondine who had by this time become immortalised in German folklore. The Undines, Paracelsus believed, were female and tended to inhabit sheltered pools and waterfalls, far from the madding crowds. The Undines liked places of peace and tranquillity, revelling in the gentle sound of the rain or the soft tinkling of the brook.

The Earth Element, according to Paracelsus, had an affinity with a group of elemental spirits called Gnomes. Gnomes, being earthy and more practically inclined, were not averse to storing up treasures on earth as opposed to heaven. They were believed to live underground or in caves – well, most of the time – and stand guard over fabulous accumulations of jewels, gold coins, etc.

Just as the association of the salamander with the Fire Element was one that really had its origin with Paracelsus, so to did the association between the Air Element and a group of spirits known as Sylphs. We don't know much about Sylphs, and even Paracelsus refrained from waxing lyrical about them. They are unknown, mysterious and of strange provenance.

Since the era of Paracelsus, the word 'elemental' has taken on a much broader meaning. Nowadays, the term *elemental* is used to describe just about any spiritual entity that is sentient or even partly-sentient. Land spirits, or 'spirits of place' are elementals that inhabit a particular geographical area and, in a sense, have a sense of ownership over the site in question. The term is also used to describe what we may call 'collective spirits' that inhabit a range of hills, a grove of trees or even a group of rock pools.

During my research, I came across a good number of experients who claimed to have had 'imaginary friends' that strongly resembled elemental spirits. It would have been easy just to discount these entities as elementals who had been wrongly labelled as QCCs, but I was struck by some cross-correspondences that led me to believe that Type 2 QCCs, whatever their nature, were closely connected to the elementals so beloved of Paracelsus. In short, I came to the conclusion that the two phenomena may well be related, possibly even having a common origin. For this reason I have included elementals – or at least, a peculiar category of them – in among my list of QCC types.

Type 2 QCCs almost always live out-of-doors, often by the coast and in remote areas where, presumably, they are unlikely to be seen. They will often be described as 'little goblins', 'pixies' or such like. Unlike Type 1 QCCs, who are always conventionally-sized, Type 2 QCCs are typically between 30 and 50 cm in height.

Type 2 QCCs tend to be named with either a double-barrelled repetitive or some other bizarre title. Mol-Mol, Koddy-Koddy, Ball Eagle and Wumpy are examples I've come across. However, there is another peculiarity about Type 2 nomenclature that needs to be pointed out here.

As we will see in later chapters, some Type 2 QCCs have double-barrelled names that are not repetitive. These may include a 'conventional' first name, such as Michael or Billy, and a more exotic second name. One experient had a Type 2 QCC called Scott Wanglie, while another informed me that hers was called Herbert Gokk. A third had a QCC – Type 2 – called John Dron.

Occasionally, the surnames of Type 2 QCCs would be conventional, including Smith, Clay and Brown. However, during my research into Type 2 QCCs, I noticed a tendency for conventional surnames to be prefixed with conventional-*sounding* first names, although in truth they weren't conventional at all. Examples include Venton Clay, Maureleen McGuire and Wilston Chang. The names Venton, Maureleen and Wilston have a superficial ring of authenticity and conventionality about them; indeed, they sound like the sophisticated names that appear in the *Times* birth announcements on a regular basis. However, they are *not* proper names.

Type 2 QCCs generally appear distant or remote to their corporeal friends. They are not exactly *un*friendly, but they don't make conversation as readily and tend not to smile very much. When pushed, however, they will occasionally offer counsel to their earthly 'charges'.

Jack Holloway recalls his relationship with a Type 2 QCC in Devon, during the 1950s:

> Pete-Pete used to appear at the bottom of my auntie's garden in Ashburton. He was always smartly dressed, and I don't recall ever seeing him wear any other colours than brown and green, although his clothing seemed to sport these colours in a multitude of shades.
>
> Pete-Pete was really nice, although he was usually very serious. He would sit and talk to me for ages, but I can't really remember specifically the details of any conversations we had.
>
> One thing about Pete-Pete I do remember is that he was obsessed with garden peas. He loved them. He would never ask for them, but there were times when I could see him looking at the pea-patch in my auntie's garden and it was obvious he wanted some. I'd say something like, 'You can take some peas, if you want', and he'd be off like a shot, eating them and filling his pockets.'

Like Type 1 QCCs, Type 2s can appear and disappear at will. However, they tend to do this less often. This may be because they inhabit remote areas where, when they are interacting with an experient, they are far less likely to be interrupted by a third party.

Jack told me that Pete-Pete would often disappear without warning, sometimes when he asked him a question about where he lived or what his family was like. 'All of a sudden he'd look very serious, and then, in an instant, he'd be gone. It was as if the question had embarrassed him, and rather than give me an open rebuttal it was easier for him just to go away for a while.'

A unique feature of Type 2 QCCs is that they may appear in multiple numbers to experients. One correspondent told me that she'd seen several Type 2 QCCs together on numerous occasions. However, only the one that she classed as her 'friend' would talk to her. The others would simply hang around in the background, watching and talking among themselves.

A number of correspondents related having brief but meaningful conversations with their Type 2 QCC. Three in particular said that they felt moved to discuss problems with them, sometimes asking for their help. The QCCs never specifically said they would help, but afterwards the experients said that their problems almost miraculously resolved themselves.

Randy James*, from Ontario, related his experience:

> My friend Gron used to appear in the woods. He was small, and had strange skin. It was shiny. He always liked to stand directly in front of me, facing me eye-to-eye. If I moved my position he would move at the same time so that we were still facing each other directly. I don't know why this was, but I wondered if he thought I was trying to trick him or attack him.

> One morning I told him that my dad's tractor was busted, and that he couldn't afford to get it fixed. When I got home, my dad said that the engine had fixed itself, but he couldn't figure how. I knew it was Gron.

Chapter eleven

Lewis and Douglas: Pennies from heaven

Sharon lives in a rural area surrounded by farms. She is married and has five children. One child, eight year-old Lewis, has a QCC called Douglas.

Five years ago, when Lewis was three, Sharon and her husband noticed that they could often hear Lewis chatting when he was upstairs. Curious, they would investigate but on each occasion would only find Lewis sitting alone with his toys. Quite naturally they assumed that Lewis was talking to himself – not an unheard of habit in youngsters of that age by any means. For some reason, however, doubts eventually crept in. It seems that Sharon and her husband weren't entirely satisfied that only Lewis's imagination was at work, for on occasion they would ask questions about these apparently one-sided conversations. However, as Sharon told me later, 'We couldn't get much out of him as he was only three.'

At around the same time, Lewis started having his conversations with apparently imaginary friends, Sharon became aware that 'strange things were occurring around the house.' As she recalled when I interviewed her, 'Things would go missing and then turn up a few days later, we'd hear tapping noises at the back door... sometimes pennies would appear from nowhere. They even fell from the ceiling on occasion.'

Readers who are reasonably well-versed in paranormal lore will already be aware that this case is already starting to sound suspiciously like a poltergeist infestation, as coins falling from the ceiling is a typical polt symptom. Regardless, neither Sharon nor anyone else in the family seems to have made a link between the rather bizarre phenomena occurring elsewhere in the house and the conversations Lewis was having in the bedroom upstairs. In fact, two years were to pass before suspicions arose that they may be connected. What exactly precipitated those suspicions was disturbing in the extreme.

Sharon's mother was visiting at the time, and while Lewis played upstairs his mother and grandmother chatted in the lounge. Suddenly, the peace was disturbed by an ear-splitting scream which Sharon described as 'simply horrible'. They both raced up the stairs to find Lewis lying on the floor under a huge pile of clothes. Naturally, Sharon and her mother wanted to know what had happened. It was at this juncture that Lewis named his assailant as 'Douglas', the allegedly imaginary friend who now didn't seem quite so imaginary after all.

According to Lewis, Douglas had experienced a bit of a temper tantrum, blamed Lewis for something and exacted punishment by hurling clothes from a nearby rail at the hapless toddler.

Many parents, even if they did suspect that 'Douglas' was in some sense real, would probably have ran away from the suggestion and preferred to live in ignorance. To her everlasting credit Sharon did not do this. Instead, she quietly sat Lewis down and asked him to tell her all about his little friend. What she heard amazed her.

First of all she managed to coax out of her son a physical description of Douglas. According to Lewis, he was seven years old (two years older than Lewis at the time) and wore, 'grey shorts, a white shirt and a funny flat cap.' There's nothing really startling about this description except for one strange thing; children don't wear flat caps now, although they did in previous generations. How could Lewis have known this? Also, the 'grey shorts and white shirt', coupled with the 'funny flat cap' clearly pictures someone right out of the pages of a Catherine Cookson novel. To me, the clothes 'hang together' too well as a period outfit – maybe from the 1930s – for them to have no basis in reality. Sharon felt the same way. 'Bear in mind this came from a five year-old who knew nothing of history.' she said in an email.

About two weeks passed by before Lewis volunteered any further information. Sharon was startled when her son told her that Douglas had actually been killed by his father. It seemed that Douglas had lived on a farm with his family, his father presumably being either the owner or the manager. One day Douglas had felt exhausted. Whether this was due to overwork, too much play or the hot weather we may never know, but at some juncture the young lad decided to take a nap. Ominously, he chose to bury himself inside a hay mound nearby. Perhaps he didn't want his father to see him sleeping. Unfortunately his father decided at that very time to work the hay and thrust a pitchfork into it vigorously. Whether young Douglas died instantly or later from his injuries we cannot tell.

Douglas and Lewis are still good friends, although Sharon doesn't pry too much. 'Even now, Lewis talks to Douglas on a daily basis and even informs us when he's not around!' she told me.

Intriguingly, Douglas is neither wholly bad nor completely good. Like most children, he behaves himself most of the time but regularly engages in mischief.

> Actually, Douglas seems pretty harmless. Sometimes he
> opens drawers and cupboards, but the only sinister
> thing he does is pull our hair and growl at times. If we
> tell Lewis off sometimes the lights dim. Lewis says this is
> him showing us he's angry.

I was still left wondering whether Sharon and her husband had actually accepted that Douglas enjoyed an objective reality. It seems to me that they have.

> Neither I nor my husband or four other children have
> seen him, but sometimes we have a strange feeling that
> we're being watched. Sometimes... sometimes we see
> things out the corner of our eye.

There are a number of aspects that make this case particularly interesting.

Firstly, Douglas is perfectly typical of conventional QCCs; almost stereotypical, one might say. If we can gain some insight into the nature and origin of Douglas then we just may get some pointers as to the nature and origin of other QCCs too.

Unlike most QCC cases, though, in this one we actually have the QCC itself informing its corporeal companion as to where it came from. Douglas had seemingly existed as a corporeal child before being accidentally killed by his father. If this is typical of all QCCs then it could be ventured with some certainty that all QCCs are simply the discarnate spirits of the dead, or ghosts, if you like. But we need to be careful. Not all QCCs are 'conventional' and a solitary case does not a solid hypothesis make.

Another strange feature of this case is the violent reaction Douglas displayed when Lewis upset him. This is certainly not typical of Type 1 QCC behaviour.

In the final analysis, all we can say is that, for the most part, Douglas behaves like any other Type 1 quasi-corporeal companion. So little research has been done into this phenomenon that our understanding of it may change radically in the years to come, and the system I have employed for categorising QCCs may become entirely redundant.

In the meantime, Douglas still plays with Lewis, thereby perpetuating the strange bond that exists between quasi-corporeal companions and their human counterparts.

Chapter twelve

Tangos in the mangoes

QCCs are almost always place-centred, and when I first began to look at the QCC phenomenon in some depth I was of the opinion that the 'place' they were attached to was quite simply a fixed geographical location, such as a house or garden. Several cases made me question this assumption, and wonder whether my concept of 'place' – at least as far as it relates to the entities in question, needed to be revised.

I interviewed a Filipino woman who, although not having had the privilege of a quasi-corporeal companion, told me that her young cousin had a Type 1 QCC that always appeared to her in a particular grove of mango trees. The cousin eventually relocated to another city, and, one day, went for a walk to familiarise herself with her new environment. Eventually, she stumbled upon a mango grove similar to the one back home where she had encountered her QCC. To her astonishment her QCC appeared and started to talk to her. This begs the question; are QCCs tied to a particular geographical location or, as it seems in this case, a particular *type* of location? Can QCCs appear not only in a set place, but also in an environment which is substantially familiar in terms of its appearance?

If the latter assumption is true, then there are a number of possible reasons for this.

Firstly, it has to be said that we know virtually nothing about the place – or places – where QCCs come from. However, we can make some broad (and, one hopes, reasonably safe) assumptions. It is likely that QCCs dwell in a dimension that is different from our own; different in nature, different in character. We may also assume that the home world of the QCC possesses dimensions of sorts, possibly including height, width and depth. It is in the nature of things that creatures and the landscapes they inhabit are mutually compatible. That is why fish live in water and worms dwell in the earth. It is probable that QCCs also follow this pattern. Whatever their world may be like, it must be one in which they dwell with a reasonable degree of contentment. It follows, then, that QCCs, like all other creatures, will gravitate naturally towards any environment where they can function well, and avoid environments which are inherently hostile to them.

Of course, creatures do not simply prefer certain environments because they are 'friendly' and they can function well in them. They also prefer environments with which they are familiar. My neighbour's lounge may be just as comfortable as my own, but I prefer to sit in my own lounge. Why? Because it is mine, I can do what I want when I want, and can relax better. It is *my* lounge. QCCs may be no different. When they traverse from their own world to ours, they no doubt choose where they want to go. They will avoid locations where they are uncomfortable, and make for places where they feel at ease. We know that they do this because of one of the habits QCCs display when they present themselves.

QCCs have a habit of appearing and disappearing at will. Many experients – the vast majority, in fact – will testify to this. That they will appear when they wish to is self-evident, but they also have a habit of disappearing when their environment changes. Typically, this will be when someone enters the environment that they do not want to be seen by or associate with. It is as if some kind of balance is being upset by the unwarranted intrusion.

Gavin Postner, from Tennessee, told me of his experiences in this regard:

> When I was just a kid I had what my pop called an 'imagination friend'. Mom and pop didn't believe that Crubbo was real, but he was.
>
> A number of times my mom or pop walked into the kitchen when Crubbo and me were playing. Crubbo would get a scared look on his face and then just disappear real quick. He wouldn't come back till mom and pop were gone.

It stands to reason, then, that QCCs have distinct preferences when it comes to the geographical locations they choose to inhabit, albeit temporarily. A change in circumstances can make them feel uncomfortable and precipitate their leaving, just as can happen with we humans. Having established a few reasonable hypotheses, then, we can now return to the Philippine mango grove and ponder once again as to why the QCC there chose to appear in two separate locations which, although geographically distant, were environmentally very similar.

The home world of the QCC may be very different indeed to ours. Truth to tell, we do not even know whether the anthropomorphic appearance of most QCCs is how they really look, or simply a guise they take on so that we humans can identify with them better. In any event, the dimension inhabited by QCCs may be so different to ours that, were we to visit it, we may find that our human senses failed to operate at all. We may not be able to see, taste, touch, smell or hear in their world. On the other hand, it is possible that the anthropomorphic appearance of QCCs may be due to the fact that that their world is very similar to ours indeed. Who knows, it may be so similar that, were we to journey there, we may find no meaningful differences between 'there' – wherever 'there' may be – and our own world. All of this is conjecture, of course; but the fact is that we have enough circumstantial evidence to suggest that when QCCs journey to this world they are selective about the places and times they visit.

When the QCC appeared to that young Filipino girl in the mango grove, it probably felt comfortable there. Perhaps the grove looked similar to part of the environment in its own world, or perhaps, over a period of time, it simply came to like that type of environment. This would possibly explain why it chose to appear to her in a very similar mango grove sometime later, even though it was in a geographically different location.

Chapter thirteen
Richard Muirhead and the
mysterious Venton Clay

Richard Muirhead is in his thirties, and has vivid recollections of his life as a child in Hong Kong before the territory was handed back to China.

From time to time, Richard and his family would holiday on Lantau Island to the west of Hong Kong. Lantau is Hong Kong's largest island, and one of its most striking features is the Big Buddha; an imposing statue which gazes out from the Po Lin (Precious Lotus) Monastery at Ngong Ping. In fact, the entire island is peppered with temples and monasteries which are dotted around its serene, beautiful landscape.

Around 1972, when Richard was five years old, he made a number of friends on Lantau Island. Interestingly none of them seem to have been *bona fide* human beings of flesh and blood. Neither do any of them seem to have been 'conventional' or Type 1 QCCs, as you will see.

The first thing that needs to be pointed out is that although Richard refers to his QCCs as 'imaginary friends' he may simply be using the phrase because it is common currency whenever the subject is discussed.

The most prominent of Richard's QCCs was a strange character called Venton (or possibly 'Vrenton', he isn't sure) Clay.

'I think Venton Clay was a bit like an elf, or possibly a gnome.' Richard told me. This of course immediately threw up the possibility that this QCC was essentially an elemental of some kind, and even now the idea cannot be lightly dismissed. In fact, even today the islanders are in the habit of leaving offerings to the tree and rock spirits. However, Venton Clay was different to Richard's other QCCs. 'He was more substantial' he added.

Alongside Venton Clay, Richard's other QCCs included characters such as 'Cheeky Tar' and 'John Dron'. To young Richard they seem to have been just as 'real' but not quite as 'substantial'. This forces us to consider a number of possibilities. It may just be that Venton Clay was not a QCC at all, but a genuine elemental spirit of some kind. Perhaps Richard's entourage of companions contained one elemental spirit and several QCCs. Another possibility is that Venton Clay was an authentic QCC, but of a different type or 'species' if you like; in fact, a Type 2 QCC.

'Conventional' or Type 1 QCCs usually have conventional names. In the UK they will be called John, Ian, Rita, Julie or Kevin. More exotic (but still conventional) names such as Tyrone, Chantelle or Cindi-Jay are rarely if ever used by Type 1 QCCs. Although the information supplied by Richard about his other friends was scant, their names alone suggest that they may belong to the Type 2 or 'Elemental' category.

Do Venton Clay, John Dron and Cheeky Tar still roam the caves of Lantau Island? Indeed they may, for it was in those same caves that Richard Muirhead first met them. If they do, may their days be happy.

Chapter fourteen
Type 3: the Animals

Type 3 QCCs look like conventional animals and are usually, but not always, proportionately-sized. Like Type 1 QCCs, they generally appear 'normal'. If you could see a Type 3 rat, dog or cat, for instance, you may never know that it was a QCC unless it suddenly disappeared in front of you. Like Type 1 QCCs, they can also appear and disappear at will.

Type 3 QCCs have a unique feature; they can almost always talk in the language of the experient and are quite happy to engage them in conversation. Intriguingly, although Type 3s usually only appear to the primary experient, they are often heard by others in the vicinity. This is interesting, for it suggests that QCCs may not be a subjective experience created in the mind of the experient, but may well enjoy some form of objective reality.

Type 3 QCCs are almost always gentle, caring and sensitive by nature. To date, I have not come across a single instance of a QCC intentionally causing harm or distress to an experient. Mind you, there is one noticeable exception to this rule-of-thumb, as we shall see presently. In that case a Type 3 QCC threatened to blow someone away with a shotgun, although mercifully the threat never materialised.

As with other QCC types, Type 3s have their own peculiarities when it comes to nomenclature. The vast majority seem to have short, monosyllabic titles such as Pik, Gef, Muk, Grof or Taj, although others will have slightly longer names such as Pebbles, Grassie and Flinker.

One of the bizarre consistencies with most QCC types is that they seem to have cultural or spiritual counterparts that are similar, but not identical, to themselves. Type 1 QCCs are often mistaken for 'ghosts' or 'spirits'. Type 2s are tantalisingly similar to the more well-known 'elemental' spirits. Type 3 QCCs have a strong cultural parallel with the notion of 'totem animals' so popular in the Native American world and the cultures of other indigenous peoples. Of course, it is indeed possible that these correspondences may cause one phenomenon to be mistaken for another. How does one know whether one is seeing the spirit of a dead child or a Type 1 QCC? Another possibility is that the two phenomena are actually one and the same, erroneously separated into two different classifications because of faulty interpretation of data.

My own feeling is that Type 3 QCCs do exist as a separate and distinct species, if you like. I have seen too much evidence – admittedly anecdotal and circumstantial – suggesting that these 'animal friends' are neither conventional beasts of the field nor spiritual 'totem animals'.

I have Indian heritage, and teach Native American culture and spirituality on a regular basis. I take the spiritual side of my life – what Indians call the Medicine Way – very seriously. For years I have worked with 'animal guides' in and from the spirit world, and I have seen nothing to suggest that Type 3 QCCs are the same phenomenon. Indeed, the differences suggest to me that they aren't.

Carol M., mentioned in chapter nine, has a friend with a Type 3 QCC. It is a horse called Pebbles. Horses are quite common Type 3s, in fact.

Like their cultural equivalents, the totem-animals, Type 3 QCCs have a tendency to dish out advice and counsel to the experients, as the following experience relates.

Alan Gates* is an ex-miner who took early retirement from the coal industry after developing a chronic back complaint. As a child, he had a Type 3 QCC called Jugg. Jugg was a dog – a Border Collie – who appeared ordinary in every sense of the word, except for two things: He could appear and disappear at will, and he could speak perfect English.

> Jugg first appeared to me when I was about three-years-old. At first I would just see him sitting there, on the rug in front of the hearth. He never made any noise – he didn't bark, or anything – and he would just look at me. He would stay for maybe five minutes, and then he would just disappear.
>
> After the first few times, he began to talk. He would maybe just say, 'Hello!' or something like that. Then he

began to talk more to me, and we would have proper conversations. I can't remember what we talked about, but I seem to recall that he would encourage me to eat my dinner, tidy my room, and such like.

Later, when I was about six – although I can't be sure – there was an incident at my school where I was beaten up by an older boy. My mother seemed to think it must have been my fault. She said I must have been cheeky to the other boy, even though I hadn't. I remember getting upset about this.

One day, around that time, Jugg came to see me. I can't recall what he said, but I remember feeling much better afterwards. I suppose he must have told me that everything would turn out alright, or something. Anyway, from that day onwards I wasn't worried at all.

About two weeks after I was beaten up, the older boy then did the same thing to someone else in my class and he got kicked out of the school. I never saw him again.

Alan never saw Jugg again until he was eight-years-old. One day, he appeared to Alan in the garden and they had a protracted conversation. Then Jugg told him that he wouldn't be able to see Alan again. Alan remembers giving Jugg a big hug. The dog then disappeared, and Alan simply got on with his life. I asked him if he missed his quasi-corporeal companion: 'Well, I suppose I did, but not as much as you might imagine. I can still remember him vividly, though.'

For the record, Type 3 QCCs have included dogs, cats, mongooses, frogs, budgerigars, snakes, horses, lions, sea lions and, would you believe, a starkly suspicious number of elephants. Apart from the elephants – and possibly horses – I must confess I haven't noticed a preponderance of any other type of creature.

On rare occasions, Type 3 QCCs have gained considerable notoriety, as we shall see in a later chapter.

Chapter fifteen

Cupboard love

I can remember clearly the first and only time that Maureen got me into trouble – big trouble. We were playing in the kitchen of our family home in Park Road, Hebburn. For some reason Maureen always seemed 'connected' to that kitchen, as if it was *her place*.

We had just had new kitchen units fitted. Whether the landlord paid for these, or my father did, I do not know; but they were very modern, in a fifties sense: white surrounds, lemon-yellow drawer fronts with clean-lined chrome handles and a mid-blue laminated work surface patterned with minute, black snowdrops.

Maureen really liked the new kitchen, and was fascinated by it. I can remember seeing her, wide-eyed, as she gazed around. 'It's *beautiful*!' she whispered, over and over again.

The kitchen was small. As you entered from the living room there was a small step down. To the immediate left there was another door, which led to a stairwell. The stairwell, in turn, led to the yard downstairs. Just past the door was the basin, and, behind it, a window which gazed down into the aforementioned yard.

The new storage units and cupboards – the most eye-catching feature of the new kitchen – were on the right as you entered. Because the units had just been installed they were largely empty. The cutlery drawer contained an assortment of knives, forks and spoons, but the cupboards beneath them were like those in Mother Hubbard's abode, quite bare.

One Friday afternoon, my maternal grandmother came to baby-sit while my mother went out shopping. For the first hour or so after lunch, I whiled away the time playing with my toys. Suddenly, Maureen appeared while my grandmother was in the 'bathroom'. Within seconds Gran left the smallest room in the house, and Maureen and I hid under the dining table in the living room. Then, at a suitable moment, we ran into the kitchen and looked for something with which we could amuse ourselves.

'Let's hide in here,' Maureen suggested, as she opened a cupboard door attached to one of our new kitchen units. Seconds later we were both sitting in complete darkness, facing each other, with our knees drawn up under our chins.

Maureen and I talked. We laughed quietly, giggled and told each other silly stories. I had no idea that my grandmother, unable to find me, was becoming increasingly alarmed. Her assumption had been, quite naturally, that I had sneaked out of the house while she was indisposed.

I discovered later that, in the grip of a blind panic, she had torn out into the street in a desperate search for her missing grandson. Just as she opened the front door, she bumped, quite literally, into my mother who had just returned from her shopping trip. Both my mother and my grandmother began to knock frantically at the doors of our neighbours nearby. The neighbours, also concerned, joined the search. Maureen and I were, of course, oblivious to the bother that we were causing.

I can't remember how long we stayed in the cupboard. It may have been half an hour, perhaps just a few minutes. My recollection is that we were under there for quite a while, but I can't be certain. However, I do remember distinctly the look of surprise on my grandmother's face as she opened the cupboard door and saw me sitting there, grinning like the proverbial Cheshire cat.

'Found him!' she bellowed, and the drama was over. To be honest, I don't even remember being scolded for my mischievousness. Maureen, of course, got off scot free.

Sometimes, when an adult entered the room, Maureen would disappear in an instant. The very presence of someone who wasn't supposed to see Maureen would trigger her disappearance in the same way that throwing a switch triggers the disappearance of the light. But this didn't happen every time. Sometimes, Maureen would just sit or stand, visible to me but not, apparently, to the adult.

At the time, I never really pondered over such incongruities. After all, I was only a child. Later, however, I would think about them deeply.

Chapter sixteen

Gef the talking mongoose

Type 3 QCCs are rarely talked about. Usually, when they raise their metaphorical head above the fortean parapet, researchers will classify them under something like, 'Curiosities', or perhaps 'Random anomalous phenomena'. Occasionally they may be labelled – wrongly, methinks – as poltergeists.

Perhaps the most famous case of this type involves a curious creature called Gef the Talking Mongoose. During the 1930s, on the Isle of Man, there lived a family called the Irvings. Their abode was a quaint farmhouse in quite idyllic surroundings – not the sort of place where a talking mongoose would seem likely to manifest its presence. Mind you, I can't think of anywhere that a talking mongoose would be *more* likely to frequent either, but that's another issue.

On Monday, 14 September, 1931, farmer James Irving was sitting at home with his wife Margaret and their thirteen year-old daughter Voirrey. Suddenly, the three Irvings heard faint but distinct noises which seemed to be coming from the vicinity of the attic. Initially, these noises sounded like animal growlings, leading the Irvings to conclude that a small mammal of sorts had perhaps taken up abode there. Curiously, though, the sounds got louder and the family agreed that they were actually listening to a voice. Although distinctly not human, they all felt that there were words wrapped up in the overall texture of the noise. Quite naturally this piqued their interest, and they strained their ears to hear more.

As if the scenario was not bizarre enough already, James Irving noticed something else. The voice – whatever its origin – was not only speaking, but actually imitating everything that the farmer was saying to his wife and daughter. Later, this aspect of the phenomenon would be likened to the way in which toddlers will try to mimic words spoken by their parents as they are learning how to talk.

With every passing sentence uttered by the voice, its command of the English language grew better. Eventually, the entity opened up to the Irvings and spouted forth what it claimed to be its life story.

Gef – as the voice called itself – had seemingly been born in Delhi, India. His birth date was Monday, 7 June 1852. This was, I may as well mention, the birth date of the eminent American plant biologist Byron David Halsted, and not very much else apart from the fact that a Mr John H Boyd laid a petition before the House of Representatives demanding the establishment of a mail route from Fort Ann to French Mountain post office, in Washington County, New York. We can safely say, then, that the first incarnation of Gef in Delhi was undoubtedly the most important thing to take place on planet Earth that day.

Gef quickly got bored with talking, though, and started to sing instead. I have heard anecdotally that, on one occasion, he even belted out *Home, Sweet Home!* which, perhaps not coincidentally, was composed by Sir Henry Bishop in the self-same year of 1852.

Gef also proved to have an economy-sized sense of humour. He would entertain the Irvings for hours with songs, cheeky poems and witty stories. However, on one occasion he solemnly declared to the family that he had not long for this world, as, alas, he had been poisoned. The Irvings were distraught, and their mood was not much lifted when Gef burst out laughing and told them that he'd been joking all along.

Gef, despite his willingness to engage the Irvings in conversational chit-chat for extended periods, was remarkably shy of letting the family see him in the flesh. Voirrey had glimpsed him on a number of occasions, but usually he'd stay hidden in the attic. From time to time he'd creep through wall cavities, and for a while even took up residence in the garden, but to Mr and Mrs Irving, Gef was still simply a disembodied voice.

It's easy to see why the epithet *poltergeist* has been used in regards to Gef. After his first introduction to the Irving family he did, it must be admitted, engage in some decidedly polt-like activity. Gef would move spoons around in the kitchen, hide articles of clothing in the broom cupboard and otherwise engage in various and sundry bits of mischief. It's unlikely that Gef meant to frighten anyone. He could be impetuous and even a little thoughtless, but the family members were unanimous in their belief that the talking mongoose was basically a canny soul.

Slowly but surely, Gef's confidence in the Irvings grew, and he started to show himself. Fleeting glimpses at first; but then, later, he'd stay for considerable periods of time.

On one occasion, Margaret Irving gently stroked Gef's fur. For some reason the mongoose jumped or moved quite quickly, and one of his teeth accidentally cut her finger. Gef was deeply upset, and immediately urged the farmer's wife to go and put some salve upon the wound. It was around this time that Gef became considerably more boisterous, and the Irvings, despite their patience, found that the animal's behaviour was becoming rather tiresome. Pleas for more restraint and decorum fell upon deaf ears, until, in desperation, the family threatened to leave. Almost instantly Gef changed, and became a very model of good mongoosian behaviour.

After a while, Gef became more and more curious about the world outside of the Irving's farmhouse. He started engaging in adventurous forays to the abodes of local neighbours, and then reporting back to the family in uncomfortable detail what they were all getting up to. Curiously, the neighbours sometimes claimed to have heard Gef – an indication that at least some in the community were disinclined to label the Irvings as mad. Mind you, there is some circumstantial evidence that the neighbours merely thought Gef to be a real-life, bona-fide mongoose which the Irvings had either purchased or adopted as a pet. Perhaps they never heard Gef speak or sing.
So then; was Gef the talking mongoose really er… a talking mongoose, or is there some other, more prosaic explanation?

One suggestion is that Gef was descended from a number of mongeese – if that's the correct collective term for a pride, gaggle or herd of mongooses, I'm not quite sure – let loose on the Isle of Man by a farmer in 1912. While it is tempting to see a connection here, I'm not convinced. If Gef was descended from the creatures released into the wild in 1912, then he was certainly no *ordinary* mongoose. This was a singing, dancing, talking mongoose unlike any other. Further, a number of wildlife experts I consulted told me that, at least currently, there are no mongooses living in the wild on the isle.

The Marsh Mongoose can still be found on the Isle of Man, although they are all enclosed in a wildlife park. Nevertheless, their existence demonstrates that the climate on the Isle of Man is favourable to at least some varieties of mongoose.

Inevitably word of Gef's existence would eventually spread beyond the Isle, and it did. The media got hold of the story, and the papers got great mileage out of what was (probably) the world's only chattering mongoose.

The family became increasingly distressed at the growing media attention, and this worried some of their friends and neighbours. One day, in 1932, a long-time family associate called John Northwood called to see how Jim, Margaret and Voirrey were faring. Gef agreed to talk to Northwood, and at first relations between the two were quite cordial. However, John seems to have upset the mongoose in some way, after which Gef issued a number of dire threats and vicious allegations towards the man. Things got worse when Northwood mentioned that his son, Arthur, was also intending to pay a visit to the Irving's farm. 'Tell him not to come! He doesn't believe!' Gef shouted loudly. 'If he does come I won't speak to him! In fact, I'll blow his brains out with a thrupenny cartridge!'

Subtle hints here, I would venture, that young Arthur Northwood may not have held pole position on Gef's Christmas card list.

Time passed, and then Gef apparently allowed Voirrey Irving to photograph him. The results were hardly spectacular, and generally show nothing more than grass and a fuzzy object of indeterminate origin. What is purported to be Gef may indeed be the talking mongoose – or possibly an old slipper.

Eventually, the affair was drawn to the attention of the legendary investigator Harry Price, who found the case irresistible and decided to launch a full-blown investigation. In late July 1935, he drew together a team of researchers and scientists and headed off for the Isle of Man post-haste.

Price, if he thought he would solve the mystery, was to be bitterly disappointed. On arrival, Jim Irving told Price that Gef had gone into hiding and had not been seen for several weeks. A few more out-of-focus photographs were taken of something wandering around in the scrub, but it was never captured or identified. In fact, some of the pictures portrayed something which looked suspiciously like a domestic cat. Price, along with magazine editor Richard Lambert, spent three days at the farmhouse along with the other researchers, but to no avail.

Price never got to see Gef at all, but there was a glimmer of hope that some concrete evidence may have presented itself. Around four months prior to his arrival, Gef told the family that he had plucked some of his own hair out and left it on the mantle shelf. This hair sample – a 'bink', perhaps? – was sent to one Captain McDonald, who happened to be good friends with Harry Price. McDonald passed on the hair to Price, who had it forensically examined. The results strongly suggested that the hair had belonged to a domestic canine. Price wanted to be sure, and retrieved from the Irving's pet dog, Mona, a further sample. In October, 1935 the results came in; alas, the hairs in the second sample proved to be identical to those in the first. All the hairs had come from Mona.

The investigator, dispirited, seemingly concluded that the talking mongoose was merely a fantasy which provided nothing more than entertainment for the Irvings. However, after Price's departure Gef returned to the farmhouse and quickly re-established his relationships with the family members. He conveniently – or perhaps inconveniently, in the cold light of history – left some footprints in the mud outside of the farmhouse. Jim Irving helpfully made casts of these and sent them off to Price, who promptly turned them over to the Natural History Museum in Cromwell Road, London.

The results of the NHM's examination were largely, but not entirely, conclusive. There were three sets of prints, each one apparently having been left by a different animal to the other two. In other words, the prints were those of three separate beasts, not one. This was deflating for those who believed in Gef, but not damning. If at least one of the sets of prints had been left by a mongoose, then there was at least some circumstantial evidence to suggest that Gef may have been more than a mere figment of the imagination.

One set of prints had, the museum said, almost certainly been made by a dog. The second set had apparently been left by a North American raccoon, although what a racoon was doing on the Isle of Man has never been satisfactorily explained. For the record, there are no raccoons currently wandering around the Isle of Man's verdant countryside, either, and the situation was no different back in the 1930s.

The third set of prints was of indeterminate origin, but the experts were able, apparently, to say with some conviction that they were not those of a mongoose.

The first question that has to be asked is whether Gef was simply a mongoose on the loose. The evidence speaks against this. There were no mongooses in the wild, and none that we know of in captivity. If Gef was a bona-fide, flesh-and-blood mongoose then he was probably the only one on the island, which simply serves to deepen the mystery even further.

Looking toward more exotic explanations, we now have to consider whether Gef was, as has been suggested by some researchers, a poltergeist of sorts.

In favour of the poltergeist explanation is the fact that Gef seemingly moved objects around the Irving household in classic polt fashion. From time to time he would also make noises that were uncharacteristic of the human-like (if not actually human) vocalisations the family had come to expect. Bangs, raps and other polty sounds would be heard by the Irvings and, occasionally, visitors to their humble abode.

But one unexpected clatter and a brace of moving tea cups do not a poltergeist make. Stacked against the poltergeist theory is the fact that Gef displayed characteristics that were decidedly *un*polt-like most of the time.

First of all, Gef talked too much. Poltergeists rarely talk, and when they do its normally in short, staccato sentences. In my experience, the talking polt – an unusual phenomenon at the best of times – normally has nothing constructive to say. One case a colleague and I dealt with proved to be the most protracted, sustained, intense (and bloody awful) polt we'd ever came across. During the course of ten months the polt spoke three times. On one occasion it threatened to throw a young child out of bed. On another it called the lady of the house a bitch, and on the third it said something totally nonsensical. Gef was different. He articulated eloquently, talked philosophically and, had he not been a mongoose, would have undoubtedly been invited to dinner parties at least twice a week.

The duration of Gef's stay at the Irving farm – several years – was also uncharacteristic of the poltergeist. Typically, a polt will hang around for a period of two to eight weeks before burning itself out. The longest polt infestation I have ever personally dealt with lasted for just over ten months.

Thirdly, Gef's personality was at variance with the typical polt, too. He was almost always described as caring and kindly, although he was known to have the odd lapse, such as the occasion he threatened to rearrange the cerebrum of Arthur Northwood with a shotgun. Polts, in my experience, are never nice. I have known them act in a friendly manner for a short period in an effort to lull their victims into a false sense of security, but I have never encountered a polt that demonstrated a caring manner for the greater period of its stay. In one case that I investigated with fellow researcher Darren W. Ritson, the polt sent a message to the householder's mobile phone from another phone that had had both its battery and SIM card removed. 'I'M SORRY. I'M GOING NOW' it said. She breathed a huge sigh of relief until the man of the house received a text message on his phone seconds later. 'I'M BACK', it declared.

Whenever a polt is seemingly nice to you, there's always a sting in the tail.

In the final analysis, there is very little about Gef to support the polt theory. However, there is another explanation that we must consider. Could the talking mongoose have been a cryptozoological creature of some kind?

Jonathan Downes, probably the UK's leading authority on cryptozoological animals, describes cryptids as 'animal species unknown to science', but he has also commented 'However, there are some "creatures" that defy categorisation within purely zoological terms of reference.' In 1990 Downes coined the term `Zooform Phenomena` to embrace these `things` (as Ivan T. Sanderson called them). Wikipedia, the free online encyclopaedia. contains a definition of zooform phenomena written by Downes:

> These are not animals at all, but are entities or apparitions which adopt or seem to have animal or part-animal form. This is where we, at least partly, enter science- fiction territory. In many ways, these elusive and contentious entities have plagued the science of cryptozoology since its inception – and tend to be dismissed by mainstream science as thoroughly unworthy of consideration. Zooform phenomena seem to be a mysterious blend of paranormal manifestation and mythological icons.

Cryptids or zooforms are not, then, ordinary animals. However, Gef did not fit comfortably within the normal definition of a cryptid, either. This leads us to consider one other possibility before we attempt to define just what sort of creature Gef was. Was it possible that someone within the Irving household was engaging in an act of deception and creating the phenomena that presented themselves for some ulterior motive?

Some investigators have pointed the finger, albeit obliquely, at John and Margaret Irving. It has been suggested that boredom may have led them to 'invent' Gef, and that they secretly delighted in the media attention they received when the case gained notoriety. Others have suggested that the hope of financial gain was in their minds, and that they possibly believed they could make a bob or two by charging visitors to tour the farmhouse where Gef allegedly resided. Of course, if guilty they wouldn't be the first people to capitalise on a predicament and turn it into a money-spinning cottage industry. However, as far as I know there is no proof that they did so. This is not to suggest that they turned down any potential gain if it was offered, but there is little evidence that they set out with this idea in mind, or engaged in some Machiavellian plot to make a fortune by deluding either their neighbours or the investigators that travelled from afar.

Next we must turn our attention to Voirrey, who was thirteen at the time when the whole affair was at its height.

What do we know about Voirrey? She was described by those who knew her as imaginative, extrovert and articulate. It has been suggested that she may have harboured some degree of dissatisfaction at her family circumstances. Her parents were retired, and apparently surviving on a meagre income of fifteen shillings per week. Voirrey, to alleviate their poverty somewhat, had taken to hunting and would regularly bring home rabbits and the like to help out. The presence of the rabbits was apparently put down to Gef rather than Voirrey, which is strange. Hunting for rabbits was not then seen as a dishonourable pastime. Why a young girl would want to blame an imaginary mongoose for filling the family larder instead of taking the credit herself is a mystery. In any event, the story goes that Mrs Irving believed Voirrey when she said that Gef was catching the rabbits, and when she told the neighbours about this then Voirrey had no choice but to carry on the deception.

Or so the story goes. Personally I doubt this. What was the point in carrying out a deception at all? And more, if one wants to deceive, why create a story that could scarcely be less believable?

A more serious challenge to Voirrey's credibility comes when one examines her interaction with Gef and, more tellingly, her activities when Gef was present.

Some researchers have pointed out that there were striking similarities between Voirrey and Gef. What Gef liked, Voirrey liked. What Gef turned his nose up at, so did Voirrey. If Voirrey was intrigued by anything – such as simple mechanics or flower arranging – then you could bet your bottom dollar that Gef would have an interest in those subjects too. Further, those who heard Gef speak said that his voice sounded very much like that of a young teenage girl. The accusations which would obviously follow such an observation are so patent that they do not require stating.

Of course, if Voirrey Irving was engaging in deception, then there are only two possibilities; her parents were either extremely stupid, or they were part and parcel of the deception themselves. The notion that Voirrey managed to deceive her parents over such a long period just doesn't fly. Besides, both Mr and Mrs Irving saw and/or touched Gef on numerous occasions. That Voirrey could have deluded her parents into thinking they could see and feel a living, talking mongoose when no such thing existed is a difficult hypothesis to sustain.

It has also been noted that Mr Irving was 'obsessed' with Gef's presence, and would talk about little else when in company. Pardon me for stating the obvious, but if I believed that my home had been invaded by a singing, talking, joke-telling mongoose then I'd probably be pretty obsessed with the situation myself.

Faced with the fact that Voirrey could hardly have sustained such an outrageous deception of her parents over such a protracted period, then, cynics are forced to conclude that the entire family was in on the act. This is a rather cruel allegation, not least because there is little or no evidence to sustain it. Hypotheses have taken on the guise of fact, unfortunately, and the characters of the Irvings have suffered because of it.

In 1937, the Irvings left their farmhouse and moved on to pastures new. Their land was sold to another farmer who, curiously, may have had an encounter with Gef himself a decade later. One day he caught sight of a 'mongoose-like animal' near the property and shot it. Some believed that the elusive Gef had finally met his end, although far more believed that Gef's residence at the farm had ended at the same time as the Irvings moved out.

Of course, much water has passed under the bridge since Gef first appeared. It is impossible to rule out fraud entirely, just as it is impossible to rule out the possibility that something truly paranormal was going on. Gef does not sit comfortably within any of the generally considered explanations for this type of phenomena, but is it possible that the talking mongoose was actually a Type 3 QCC?

Let us look at some of the characteristics of Gef. Firstly, we know that he could not have been a conventional mongoose. Mongooses simply don't talk, sing and crack witty one-liners. This in itself makes Gef, at least potentially, a candidate for inclusion in the list of QCC species.

Gef was also helpful, offering counsel and practical advice to the Irvings. This is also a feature of QCCs.

There are aspects of Gef's behaviour that are not typical of QCCs. Although Voirrey Irving was undoubtedly the 'focus' in the affair, she was far older than the typical QCC experient. Gef was also unusual in that he allowed himself to be seen and heard by others apart from the principal experient. There again, nothing in the world of paranormal research is an exact science, so perhaps we shouldn't be surprised.

The truth of the matter is that too much water has passed under the bridge for us to say with any certainty just what Gef was. However, I believe he fits – albeit awkwardly – better into the 'quasi-corporeal companion' mould than any other.

Chapter seventeen

Can you help me, Sergeant Major?

Caroline Corfield read my letter in the *Fortean Times*, and generously offered me her own experiences. When Caroline was little she had, by her own admission, several 'imaginary' friends. One of them, bizarrely, was a sergeant major in the British Army. She confided that this may have been inspired by a film she saw as a youngster in which Shirley Temple apparently took the part of 'the daughter of a British soldier stationed in India.' In all probability, this was *Wee Willie Winkie* (1937), staring the legendary Cesar Romero who took the part of the rebel leader Khoda Khan. C. Aubrey Smith took the role of Shirley's grandfather, not her father, but in every other respect the movie seems to be the one that Caroline remembers.

But Sergeant Major was not Caroline's only QCC. He was accompanied by half a dozen or so 'naughty sailor boys', whose behaviour was not always the epitome of decorum. Caroline has strong visual memories of a number of events that took place during her childhood where her 'imaginary' friends paid her a visit. Some of these incidents took place when she was little more than one-year-old. Her remembrances also include clear recollections of what her QCCs looked like:

> I remember them being the same size as myself at the time. A much-reminisced scene is when my bucket and spade fell between the train and the platform while going on holiday, and I said it was the naughty sailor boys, who my mum had to tell off there and then, much to the amusement of passing passengers. I vaguely recall a conversation with my 'friends' about what would happen to something that went in between the platform and the train prior to whatever happened next. Sorry, but I can't seem to remember how the bucket and spade got between the train and platform, although it's a shrewd guess I threw them there.

Perhaps, but the case illustrates how many experients find the presence of their QCCs difficult to deal with when they intrude in 'real life' scenarios; particularly when adults are around who may not be as ready to accept the existence of QCCs as readily as children do.

Caroline went on:

> My sister was three years younger than myself, and the memories of these friends evaporated as she became my playmate instead. The quality of reality for these friends was much the same as for the animation of my favourite teddy bear.'

Cynics will point to Caroline's testimony as proof-positive that QCCs are, as has long been argued, simply substitutes for 'real' playmates. When the 'real' playmates come along, then the 'imaginary' ones simply walk off into the metaphorical sunset, never to be seen again.

Caroline now has children of her own, with a much smaller gap between them than the one that existed, age-wise, between her and her sister. To date, none of them have mentioned having any quasi-corporeal companions.

Caroline still finds certain aspects of her experience with QCCs hard to grasp. 'It is amazing,' she voices, 'how the reality of an animate teddy can still be felt even by an adult. I hope this [writing about her experience] helps. I can always dredge up more stories if you need, a quick talk with my mum will produce many more embarrassing situations I put her in.'

Was the existence of Caroline's 'sergeant major' really precipitated by a Shirley Temple film? Who can say? Regardless, she possessed a number of quasi-corporeal companions who certainly had an impact upon her life and the way she views the world around her.

Chapter eighteen
Type 4: the Wackies

'Wackies' comprise the fourth and most heterodox species of quasi-corporeal companion. Even for fortean researchers of great fortitude and broadness of vision, their existence can be hard to swallow.

Wackies seem to come in two distinct types: the Sages and the Animates. Like other types they have the ability to appear and disappear at will, but their most incongruous appearance sets them apart from the others.

'Sages' are human-like, but typically dress in an exotic manner and tend to display distinct cultural characteristics. Almost always, these differences will encapsulate a culture different to that of the experient. They may appear as a Native American warrior, a Hindu-like sage or a Chinese mandarin, etc. Sages may also only show themselves from the waist up (one youngster told me that his 'Eskimo' QCC would appear from the waist up at floor level, looking as if his legs were buried in the ground.) Sage-like Wackies always appear as adults, never children. This also sets them apart from the more common Type 1 variety. Typically they will dispense pearls of wisdom to their young experients, often urging them never to steal, get angry or hurt others. Type 4 Sages are almost always benevolent.

'Animates' share many of the characteristics of Sages, but their appearance is radically different. Curiously, Animates will appear as everyday household objects that suddenly grow arms and legs (but rarely heads). During my research I've came across yoghurt cartons, banana skins, wall-mounted radiators and candle-holders which have suddenly taken on a life of their own and spoken to their undoubtedly startled witnesses.

Like other orders of QCC, Type 4s will either have human names such as Walter, Ethel or Cindy, or, again, double-barrelled repetitives like Mook-Mook, Kobby-Kobby or Fudda-Fudda. This common denominator, perhaps more than any other, urges me to include 'animates' within the family tree of quasi-corporeal companions.

One characteristic typical of Type 4 Sages and Animates is that they usually only appear when the experient is at a low ebb psychologically. When the child experient is unhappy, worried or depressed a 'sage' will appear or a nearby object will burst into life, grow arms and legs and offer words of comfort.

Animates have a curious habit of leaving behind essentially useless 'gifts' for experients, such as a pile of biscuit crumbs on the carpet, a small ball of coloured fluff or a dried leaf. Carol M., you will recall, was often gifted 'binks' by her quasi-corporeal companion, Fred.

All four types of QCC that I've identified seem to have a penchant for dishing out advice; however, there are distinct differences between both the quality and the quantity of the counsel proffered. Type 1 QCCs look like children, and they speak like them too. Rarely do they offer advice that would seem to be beyond that normally within the abilities of someone commensurate with their age. Maureen, I recall, once told me not to turn the tap on in the kitchen too quickly, 'because the water will come shooting out.' Elizabeth once told me not to eat my sandwiches before washing my hands, 'because people who eat food with dirty hands are horrid.' Type 1 QCCs seem to possess a level of insight in keeping with their appearance. They look – and talk – like children. I do not recall coming across a classic Type 1 case in which the QCCs engaged their experients in philosophical dialogue or chat about the meaning of life, the universe and everything. As with 'real' children, such deep stuff is seemingly beyond them.

Type 2 QCCS, the Elementals, seemingly possess a much deeper understanding of the world. They are not so chatty as Type 1 QCCs, and tend to possess far more reserved personalities. However, when pushed they will usually offer philosophically-charged advice to the experients.

Type 3 QCCs, the Animals, often act like unpaid nannies or substitute parents. They will scold their charges for misbehaving, encourage better behaviour and urge them to take responsibility for their actions. They will sometimes wax lyrical, but are more likely to crack jokes or make wry observations than to engage in deep conversation over profound issues.

Type 4 Sages are the most philosophical of the QCC species. They will often sound, when dispensing advice, as if they are quoting scripture or repeating the words of a spiritual guru.

Glen Smith* told me of his own experience with a Type 4 Sage called Edwinn. (I asked Glen why he spelt Edwinn with a double *nn*, and he told me that that was the way that his QCC insisted he spell it.)

Edwinn was a Spanish Conquistador who always appeared in full battle-dress and holding a spear in his left hand. He would appear in the living room, in front of an antique oak cabinet, with the lower half of his body buried beneath floor level.

Glen told me how, on one occasion, Edwinn appeared to him just days after his maternal grandmother had died and he was missing her terribly.

> Suddenly he was there, by the cabinet as usual. I can remember that his breastplate and helmet were shining brightly. I think he must have polished them constantly.
>
> He asked me why I was unhappy, and I told him about my grandma dying. He said, 'You know, the more you watch the clock, the happier you'll feel. You will never forget your grandmother, but in time you won't cry as much. Remember, Glen; the more you watch the clock, the happier you'll be.
>
> I was only eight or nine at the time, and I couldn't understand what Edwinn meant. How would watching the clock stop me being upset about my grandma dying? Anyway, I tried it out. I sat watching the large clock on the living room wall for ages, and in a weird sort of way it worked. I've never forgotten my grandma, but the simple act of staring at the clock on the wall helped me. Just don't ask me how.

There are a number of possible explanations for why Edwinn may have made this bizarre suggestion to young Glen, and intriguingly, a number of reasons as to why this rather unusual form of grief-counselling may have worked.

It struck me as interesting that Edwinn urged Glen to 'watch the clock', and I wondered whether this other-worldly Conquistador had actually got the youngster to engage in a little bit of self-hypnosis. Was powerful autosuggestion at work here? With every rhythmic tick of the clock hands, was Glen convincing himself that he would quickly recover from the loss of his beloved grandmother?

Another possibility is that Edwinn was trying to get Glen to understand a concept really only grasped by adults; that, after the loss of a loved one, time *really is* a great healer.

I was very close to all four of my grandparents, and was very lucky to have them all with me well into adulthood. The first to die was my maternal grandmother, the others following her into the next life over a period of eighteen years. After the death of each I felt an acute sense of loss, but, with the passage of time, I healed. Eventually it became possible to think of them without shedding tears.

Of course, saying to an eight or nine year-old, 'Time is a great healer' would be completely fatuous. They just wouldn't *understand* the great truth behind the words, let alone take comfort from them. However, if we were to say to a grieving youngster, 'You know, the more you watch the clock, the happier you'll feel. You will never forget your grandmother, but you won't cry as much. Remember; the more you watch the clock, the happier you'll be,' it's just possible that they'd get the point. What Edwinn did here, perhaps, was to reduce a little bit of homespun philosophy into a form that a child could grasp more readily. Whatever Edwinn's reasoning, the tactic worked.

On another occasion, Glen got very upset when a schoolteacher blamed him for something he hadn't done. Glen was punished, and his mother got to hear about the affair. Glen protested his innocence, and eventually Mrs Smith went up to the school to sort matters out. Glen takes up the story:

> When my mother went into the class to see the teacher,
> she told him that I was claiming I hadn't broken the
> chair. I remember her saying, 'You know, I know when
> Glen's lying, and I'm sure he's telling the truth.'

'I'll never forget what the teacher did next. He smiled and ruffled my hair with his hand, then he said, 'Mrs. Smith, don't be too hard on the lad. He's obviously frightened at the thought of being punished. The thing is, I *saw* him throw that chair across the room with my own eyes.'

I got the detention, and I also got punished at home for 'embarrassing' my mother. I hated that teacher. I *knew* I hadn't broken the chair, and therefore I *knew* he couldn't have seen me. He was lying, but had made out to my mother that he almost felt sorry for me and had really let me off lightly. What a nasty bastard he was; I hated him for that. I later found out that it was another pupil in my year who had broke the chair. I also found out that he was the teacher's nephew.

The day after the incident in question, Edwinn appeared again. Glen remembers distinctly what he said: 'Glenn, worry not when others speak ill of you. In time, their lies will pierce them like an arrow.'

I asked Glen how old he was when this incident took place, and he said he was eleven; quite old for a QCC experient. I also asked him if he'd fully understood what Edwinn had said, given the fact that his language on that occasion had been flowery and ornate.

> Yes, I understood him quite clearly. I knew straight away what he was saying; that the teacher was going to suffer for what he did, that his lies would come back to haunt him.

And did they, I enquired?

> Well, in a way. Another teacher found out who had really broken the chair and there was some sort of investigation. The teacher who lied about me said that he must have been mistaken, as 'the two boys look very alike'. Actually, we looked nothing like each other, and everyone knew it. Nothing ever happened to the teacher, but everyone knew he had lied to protect his nephew. I think the embarrassment was a real punishment for him. My mother demanded – and got – a letter of apology.

By far the most curious QCC sub-species is that of the Animates. Their function seems to be similar to that of the Sages, but during my research I found that their advice and counsel possessed a more practical aspect to it, whereas the Sages tended to be distinctly philosophical in their approach. I also found that Animates tend to have a much shorter shelf-life than Sages and other types of QCC. Some only appear once, while others will usually pay their charges two or three visits at the most.

Jane McCloud related her experience with an Animate:

> When I was a child I had an imaginary friend called Mr Poker. I think I invented the name, because that's exactly what he was: a poker.
>
> On the hearth in the lounge my mother and father had a small, brass stand which housed a brush, a shovel and a poker. One day, I was lying on the rug near the fire

reading a comic when the poker spoke to me. I got quite a shock. It just said, 'Hello!' and that was that. I didn't tell my mother and father, because I knew they wouldn't have believed me.

A few days later the poker spoke to me again. I was listening to the radio – again, in the lounge – when the presenter said something about the actress Diana Dors dying. At this point I heard the poker say 'Hello' again, and I looked over to the hearth. The poker was no longer on the stand. I couldn't believe what I was seeing. It had grown two legs and was standing on the hearth itself.

I asked the poker what it wanted. It said, 'We all have to go sometime', and then said, 'But you have other things to worry about. Your mum asked you to do the dishes, and you've forgot. Forget Diana Dors and get the dishes done.

Mr Poker was always reminding me of things I'd forgotten, and the funny thing was that I never once questioned my sanity or thought I was going mad. I just accepted that our poker could talk, and that was it.

I asked Jane how many visits she'd had from Mr Poker in his animated state, and she estimated around five or six – slightly higher than the normal number. The poker itself stayed in the family for years, but never 'burst into life' after the last visit, which took place when Jane was ten years old.

Chapter nineteen

Hi-Ho, Pebbles

Lorraine is a close friend of Carol M., mentioned in an earlier chapter. She also had an imaginary friend – a horse called Pebbles.

Lorraine's Type 3 QCC first made an appearance when Lorraine was around two-years-old. He played, she remembers, 'a large part in my life while he was with me'.

At this juncture we need to point out something about Type 3 QCCs. Those that appear in the guise of domesticated animals, such as dogs, cats and budgerigars, tend to appear indoors, whereas larger Type 3s, such as elephants and horses, almost always appear out of doors. This fact is interesting, for it precipitates some intriguing questions.

By their nature, QCCs are bizarre and follow few of the rules which govern how we flesh-and-blood humans live our lives. And yet, Type 3 QCCs almost always appear in places where their fleshly, conventional counterparts would usually be found. Could it be that Type 3 QCCs, which are usually the only species to appear to multiple experients – albeit extremely rarely – appear as 'normal' animals in 'normal' places so that even if they are seen by others their appearance is less likely to draw attention? A normally-proportioned pig in a pen will cause little in the way of consternation, while a miniature pig that suddenly appears in a hamster cage will probably raise an eyebrow or two.

Like most non-domesticated Type 3 QCCs, Pebbles lived outdoors. Her normal home was at the bottom of the garden, where Lorraine would spend hours cleaning, grooming and feeding him.

Lorraine recalls that she, 'nearly drove my family daft, as I would insist that they had to hold his rein at shoulder height. This meant that they would have to walk around with their hand in the air. This proved to be very embarrassing for my older sister, who was about thirteen or fourteen at the time.

'Pebbles was dapple grey and went everywhere with me. On one occasion I made my sister take me back on the bus to the stop where she had left him.' Whether Lorraine's sister could actually see and interact with Pebbles, or whether she was simply teasing Lorraine by claiming to have left Pebbles at a bus stop, we do not know. However, it is intriguing to see how the presence of Pebbles not only affected Lorraine directly but also, indirectly, the other members of her family.

Lorraine says that she can't remember when Pebbles departed from her, but her story has an interesting post-script. Lorraine had a close friend whom she played with on a regular basis. Frequently they seem to have invented 'imaginary beasts', which were usually 'large cats'. 'Whenever we played, these animals could talk and had powers that would help us in whatever quest we took on.'

These beasts, I would venture, were of a radically different nature to Pebbles. The ability to call upon 'totem animals' or 'power animals' is well known in many indigenous spiritual cultures. These animals can be trained to appear specifically when we are about to journey on a 'quest' of some kind, and my belief is that this was exactly what Lorraine and her friend were doing.

Richie Appleton also had a Type 3 QCC; a horse called Grot. Grot lived in a field next to Richie's home in Idaho. The field also contained many conventional horses, but Grot could only be seen by Richie.

> I guess my parents couldn't see him at all. When the other horses were galloping around the grass, Grot would come over and let me feed him off my hand. My dad used to complain that I was wasting feed because it just spilled onto the dirt, but in my mind it didn't. Grot ate everything I ever gave him. To me Grot was feeding, but to my dad the feed was just spilling onto the ground.

Grot would sometimes talk to Richie.

> He'd tell me stuff, you know... like how I should do my homework, clean up the yard... but he was never demanding. One day, I noticed that another horse in the field had a game leg. Grot told me not to worry, that she'd be okay. She was.

Chapter twenty

Erica and Mr He

Erica Thomas saw my letter in the *Fortean Times* and contacted me about her own QCC experience.

As a child, Erica had a Type 2 QCC called Mr He. Like other Type 2s, he lived outdoors in the garden.

Erica remembers something distinctly unusual about Mr He; he – no pun intended – 'had the knack of changing the colour of his garments to match his surroundings.' (Martin Jackson, another correspondent, told me that his Type 2 QCC could do exactly the same thing, which is intriguing.)

Erica continues:

> My mother [Patricia Watts] was quite a good amateur
> poet, and on my fourth birthday she gave me a
> collection of verses she had written for me, including
> one about Mr He.

Erica kindly sent me a copy of the poem, which is reproduced below, in full:

Mr He

Hush! Keep still! There's Mr He
Peeping round the apple tree.
Out of the corner of my eye
His tasselled cap I chanced to spy.
Don't let him know we know he's there,
Just look as if you didn't care.
How warm the sun, how green the trees.
How hot we'd be without this breeze!
You've never heard of Mr He?
Most every day he plays with me.
He's small and quick and very shy
With sparks and twinkles in his eye.

Perhaps he's young, or maybe old,
And dressed in green or brown or gold.
It all depends on where he stands;
Green on the grass, gold on the sands,
Brown where the leaves of autumn whirl,
White where the feathery snowflakes swirl.
He's very fond of lupin seeds,
For that's the sort of food he needs,
And hazel-nuts, and honey sweet
From clover blooms he loves to eat.
He's never sad, but always gay
From early morn to close of day.
Look! There he is on the rockery,
Green as a fern and twinkling at me.
Why can't you see him? He's quite plain.
Look quick, or he'll be gone again!
Now it's too late, he's vanished quite.
Grown up folks have shocking sight!

Erica's mother may have done researchers a greater service than she could ever have imagined, for her quite beautiful poem allows us to see how thoughtful adults can, if so minded, approach the entire QCC enigma in an extremely positive way.

Firstly, she makes reference to the fact that Mr He possessed chameleon-like abilities, blending in with the background scenery perfectly. This begs the question as to whether some QCCs – or maybe even all of them – actually utilise this mechanism as a means of appearing and disappearing at will. Perhaps when QCCs disappear they don't actually 'go' anywhere, but merely make themselves invisible by adapting themselves to the appearance of the local environment in an extraordinary manner.

Erica's mother, like all poets, allowed herself a degree of artistic licence. In the poem she writes, 'He's very fond of lupin seeds, for that's the kind of food he needs / And hazel nuts, and honey sweet from clover blooms he loves to eat.' Beautiful rhyme, filled with the innocence of childhood; but Erica wasn't entirely happy. 'I can still remember my sense of outrage to find that, although I liked the poem on the whole, she had got one bit seriously wrong. I knew that Mr He existed solely on lupin seeds and would have really *hated* the nuts and honey!'

Over the Wall

*A Medley of Verse
for Young Folk*

Patricia Watts

The cover of one of Patricia Watts'
books of poems

During my research I found that those who experience all types of QCC seem to have a peculiar eye for minutiae and become irritated when others deliberately or inadvertently get it wrong. When an experient says that his QCC wore a fawn-coloured jacket, then woe betide anyone who describes it as sand-coloured, brown or khaki.

Erica confided that her eldest daughter also had a QCC when she was a child. Details of his appearance are sketchy, but there are some indications that he may have been a Type 4 Sage. Gatty, Erica told me, 'spent his entire life sitting on a piece of wood in the engine room.'

This requires some explanation. Erica and her family lived in a houseboat on the Thames, which had originally been a Second World War motor torpedo boat. The (empty) engine room eventually became a spacious lounge, but at this time it was pitch dark, had no floor and was rather spooky.

'Why Gatty chose to live there, I can't imagine', Erica acknowledges. 'When my second and later third daughters arrived, Gatty moved out.

I have a theory that imaginary friends only visit solitary children. What do you think?'

Like many people, Erica seemed to be taken with the notion that 'solitary children' are the prime experients in QCC cases. I believed this at one time, but, as previously detailed, it is simply not the case.

Erica has some other thoughts about Gatty, and the QCC phenomenon in general:

> I don't know what Gatty's diet was like, but with Mr He I think the lupin seed connection may have been that they are rather like tiny peas, and I used to like shelling them.

Lupin seeds are also quite poisonous, of course, which tells us that QCCs are not bound by the same laws of chemistry as humans when it comes to ingesting toxic substances.

Despite the captivating nature of these stories, Erica says that she 'can't really take on board the fact that Mr He and Gatty existed anywhere but in my and my daughter's imaginations. However, one must keep an open mind.'

Quite. But before we depart from the world of Mr He and Gatty, we need to return once more to the poem penned by Erica's mother.

It is quite remarkable that Erica's mother accepted – nay, tentatively encouraged – her daughter's relationship with Mr He. She did not become overly concerned, seek psychiatric help or scold Erica; she gracefully accepted that Mr He, whatever his true nature and origin, had entered her daughter's life and, in some strange way, enriched it. Her poem gives a beautiful gloss to Erica's experience, and if all other parent's did the same we may be far closer to explaining this enigma than we are at present.

Chapter twenty-one
Elvis has entered the garden

My appeal for further QCC experiences in the *Shields Gazette* brought a response equal to that gained by my request in the *Fortean Times.* One correspondent, Kay Johnson, related to me her experience with a Type 4 Sage known – wait for it – as Elvis:

> I read your article about imaginary friends in the *Shields Gazette*, and thought I'd write and let you know about my own experience. I'm a 19 year-old girl now, but when I was around 4 I had an imaginary friend called Elvis.
>
> I don't remember a whole lot about him now, but I do recall that he always wanted to dance with me, and that he lived in my grandmother's garden.
>
> I have one very vivid memory of dancing with him in the garden – he was twirling me under his arm and we were laughing and eating sweets.
>
> Okay, here comes the really strange part. As I've said, my imaginary friend was called Elvis. He looked like an exaggerated version of Elvis Presley just before he died. I remember him wearing one of those white jump suits with all the gems on it and he was really overweight. This might not be strange if it weren't for the fact that, at four-years-old, I had absolutely no knowledge of the real Elvis Presley. No one in my family was an Elvis fan (not even my grandmother, who's garden my 'imaginary friend' lived in), so I'd never even come into contact with a piece of Elvis memorabilia.
>
> My parents didn't think anything strange about it until a few years later, when I was watching TV with them and an image of the real Elvis Presley came on the screen. I pointed at the TV and said 'That looks like Elvis.'

This probably sounds made up, or you might even think I'm crazy, but I assure you this is totally true. There are a lot of people in my family who can all remember me playing and talking to Elvis and none of them knew where I'd gotten the name from (I don't even remember that).

My grandmother told me that one day I was playing with Elvis in the garden and her neighbour asked her 'Who is Elvis? Is he is a cat or something?' and she just replied 'Oh no, it's her imaginary friend!' She even remembers one time when I was making him his breakfast and calling for him to eat it before it got cold.

I don't really remember what happened to Elvis, but as I got older he just stopped showing up. To this day no one in my family can explain where I got the image of Elvis from. There was really no way, at four-years-old, for me to have any kind of knowledge of the real Elvis Presley, the kind of clothes he wore and the fact that he was overweight.

I hope this is useful to you and I hope you don't think I'm too mad! I swear this is all true.

And I have no reason to disbelieve Ms Johnson at all, for her account bears almost all of the hallmarks of a typical Type 4 Sage encounter.

Most Type 4 Sages are culturally stereotypical in appearance; 'the Red Indian', the Pirate', 'the Chinese Mandarin', and so on, but they cannot usually be identified as paralleling a specific person. Elvis was different, because he obviously looked – and dressed – like a recently-deceased rock star.

Elvis, we must presume, wasn't really Elvis, if you get my drift; not unless the deceased have the ability to return as quasi-corporeal companions. This is important, for it may indicate that QCCs, or at least this type, have the ability to present themselves in a way that does not mirror their true appearance. Perhaps they take on an appearance that their young experients can, in some unfathomable way, identify with or at least accept comfortably.

This may also explain the way in which Type 4 Sages appear so regularly in culturally stereotypical forms. I find it hard to believe that, in the netherworld QCCs actually inhabit, there are legions of Chinese Mandarins, Hindu Gurus, Cowled Monks and feathered-up Indian Chiefs all queuing up to make their appearance in our own world. A percentage of QCCs, then, may be what they seem to be, but not really look like they appear.

Chapter twenty-two

For you, Tommy...

Karisha* responded to my appeal in the *Shields Gazette* with an intriguing tale of her own Type 1 QCC called Tommy.

Karisha has two sisters, whom she describes as 'both more than eleven years older than me'. As she was somewhere around the age of four or five when she had her own QCC experience, then her sisters would both have been in their teenage years. Superficially, this would lend some credibility to the idea that 'lonely children' invent QCCs to counteract the diminishing interaction with their siblings. As Karisha's sisters gained increasing independence, perhaps they spent less and less time with their little sister. Perhaps, then, Karisha 'invented' Tommy to cure a degree of boredom.

Well, that's how the theory goes, but I don't buy it. Karisha's correspondence demonstrates that she was close to her sisters. More than that, her siblings were inexorably drawn into 'Tommy's world', and forced to interact with him in a way that Karisha even now describes as 'embarrassing'.

Karisha can't recall too much about Tommy's physical appearance, but she does remember that, 'he was the same age as me and just a normal boy.' Like most Type 1 QCCs, Tommy was reasonably good-humoured. Karisha recalls fondly that he would make her laugh, and would sit for hours playing games with her. Karisha and her family members can now only remember 'clips' of the times she spent with Tommy. Those they can remember make interesting reading:

> Once, on a shopping trip, one of my sisters left Tommy sitting on the counter in a shop. Well, obviously, I can remember being distraught until they went back for him!
>
> When he went shopping with us they had to hold his hand, and my mam remembers when she once left him

on the bus. Once again I was inconsolable! She also had to set his place at the table for dinner!

I loved Tommy. He was my best friend for ages, and he was there 24/7 with me.'

But what about Tommy's origins? Karisha offers a suggestion: I guess he came from me being the youngest child, and with both parents being at work.' Again, the almost universally accepted explanation for QCCs vouches forth. However, as in other cases, Tommy may have a far greater degree of 'reality' than Karisha or her family imagines. Karisha said she didn't mind at all if I included her story, which was kind of her. 'I'm just glad to hear other people's stories about their own experiences, because I thought it was just me!'

This is another strange feature of the QCC phenomenon. During the early days, when experients see nothing weird or abnormal about the presence of their quasi-corporeal companion, they tend to assume that every other child 'has one'. Then, as time goes on and the experients become aware that there is something unusual indeed about their companion – such as the fact than no one else can see them – their perception changes. Experients start to believe that no one else has such a friend. Not only is the QCC unique among the experient's circle of friends, but the *experient* believes they are unique in having such a peculiar companion.

Karisha promised to send me any other details if they came to mind, and she was as good as her word. These postscripts to her story are also fascinating, and demonstrate that, no matter how imaginary QCCs may seem to adults, they are *very* real to the experients. 'My mam's just reminded me of the time when we were travelling on the bus. She actually sat on Tommy, at which point I just turned and screamed!' Karisha also mentioned that Tommy's favourite meal was spaghetti bolognese.

Perhaps the most remarkable feature of Karisha's story is her recollections of the times when Tommy was left behind in a store, left behind on a bus, and so on. Most times, but not always, her sisters were responsible. There is an extraordinary parallel here between this case and that of the aforementioned Pebbles, the Type 3 QCC of Lorraine, when Pebbles the horse was left at a bus stop by the experient's sister.

Luc Badeau, from Normandy, had a Type 1 QCC who, funnily enough, but maybe not coincidentally, was also called Luc. Luc Badeau's QCC was once left on a train when the family were journeying to Paris. Luc recalls:

> I was hysterical. I cry all the time for Luc, but my mother would not go back. One time, my sister left Luc at the pharmacy and I was very upset. I go looking for him, but I could not find him. When I return, he is already home – and very cross with my sister.

Numerous correspondents recalled times when family members accidentally (one hopes) 'lost' their QCCs. In all cases that I'm aware of, the QCC eventually made it home.

Of course, there is an obvious explanation for this pattern. QCCs are almost always only visible to their experient. Hence, when the QCC travels out of doors with the experient and one or more family members, understandably all but the experient could easily 'forget' that the QCC is with them, because they may not really believe that the QCC really exists in the first place.

Plausible though this theory is – and it's probably the correct explanation in the majority of cases – there are a number of peculiar trends within the 'lost QCC' scenario that are intriguing.

Firstly, in an unusual number of cases it is the female sibling or siblings of the experient who accidentally lose the QCC outdoors. Secondly, in almost all cases the QCC is 'lost' or 'forgotten' on a shopping expedition. Thirdly, the QCCs are almost always lost either in a store or on public transport. Currently I have no explanation whatever for these common denominators, but if anyone has I'd like to hear from them.

Chapter twenty-three

Dem bones, dem bones...

Louise Driggers lives in France. As a child she had a Type 4 Animate QCC called Ebert, although there is a slight question mark over his exact classification within the QCC family tree of species.

Louise had read my letter in the *Fortean Times*, and emailed me with her own, pre-school experience with a QCC. Ebert was a skeleton who, as is the wont of some quasi-corporeal companions, lived in a radiator.

A skeleton is the internal framework of most creatures, bar those that, like insects and spiders, have an exoskeleton. This leads us to ask whether Ebert was actually a Type 1 QCC who was remarkably devoid of flesh, or something else altogether; perhaps, as I've suggested, a Type 4 Animate. I've plumped for the latter, but if I receive any complaints from the Board of QCC Control or the Amalgamated Union of Wackies, then I'll be quite happy to amend further editions of this book.

Unlike some QCCs, Ebert enjoyed 'celebrity status' in Louise's family. She thinks, perhaps correctly, that this was because 'a skeleton was considered a strange thing for a little girl to latch on to.' No argument there, although Louise's husband thinks her experience was 'sweet but crazy', and 'maintains that I must have been as eccentric a child as I am an adult.'

Louise says that she doesn't 'remember ever talking to Ebert, but I knew he was there, and we obviously "communicated" somehow as my stories would be quite detailed.' As mentioned earlier, the inability of experients to remember the exact nature of conversations with their QCCs is common.

Louise found her interaction with Ebert to be positive, but in the strangest of ways.

> 'I think the true legacy of Ebert is that I have never found skeletons or skulls to be in the least bit

frightening. People who screamed at ghost trains baffled me as a child.'

I received correspondence from other experients who had similar tales to tell. James White, from Colorado, had a Type 2 QCC called Bollots – careful how you pronounce that – who was acutely aware of James' fear of dogs. Whenever James had an unpleasant canine encounter, Bollots would always show up with something like a Doberman or a German Shepherd in tow. 'They were always real friendly, and Bollots would get me to stroke them. Pretty soon I stopped being afraid of dogs.'

It's hard not to imagine that Bollots was, in some way, acting as a therapist here and helping James to overcome his fear of dogs by exposing him to them. Just what encourages QCCs to engage in this sort of behaviour, wherein they help their charges through a wide variety of psychological crises, is a mystery. But they do.

Chapter twenty-four

Gumby and Bongabeers

Paul Dale is in his thirties and lives in the delightful village of Haworth, West Yorkshire. Paul had two QCCs as a child, and they were highly unusual as – almost unheard of in Types 1, 3, and 4 cases – they always appeared together. However, their appearance – more about that momentarily – gives the game away that they were indeed Type 2 QCCs, in which cases multiple appearances are not that uncommon.

Gumby and Bongabeers were not twins, however, as their physical appearances were distinct from each other. Gumby was only two feet in height, thin and usually turned up in a green suit. Bongabeers was the same height, but slightly more corpulent. His normal attire was a beige pullover and brown britches. Gumby, Paul says, was 'the most dominant character'. Paul told me that he had, 'no idea where their names came from. A few years ago I found out that there was an American (cartoon?) character named Gumby, who is green, but I do not recall seeing this character when I was young.'

On a whim, I decided to do some detective work and see what – if anything – I could find out about the origins of these two QCC names. Ye gads, I wish I'd never started. Gumby was a roughly anthropomorphic figure, green in colour, and carved out of clay, who starred in no less than 223 episodes of an American TV series over a period of thirty-five years beginning in 1955. Since then he has been the subject of movies, games and other media related enterprises and is still popular with kids and adults alike. Do a search on 'Gumby' on the Internet, and you'll see how much information I had to trawl through to find out more about this loveable little rascal. According to Gumbyphiles, his creator named him after a slang term used in Michigan to describe muddy, waterlogged roads. Sodden tracks and pathways were apparently known collectively as 'the gumbo'.

Bongabeer was harder to track down. A search on the name as Paul Dale spelt it produced nothing, but separating the word into two separate ones – *bonga* and *beer* – proved to be enlightening. Bonga beer was, apparently, a cannabis-laced beverage popular in the Orient many centuries ago.

Of course, the similarities between the Gumby of American cinematographic fame and his slightly less well-known counterpart in Haworth may be entirely coincidental, although the fact that Paul Dale's Gumby wore a green suit, and the US version was also green in colour, may be significant. I doubt it, though. In any event Paul cannot remember seeing the American Gumby on TV – or anywhere else for that matter.

The chances that Paul's Bongabeer was named after an obscure Oriental nightcap is also unlikely, but in the weird world of the quasi-corporeal companion, nothing can be ruled out entirely.

Unlike other QCC types, Type 2 Elementals are not keen on breaking their fast in the presence of their corporeal companions. Whereas Type 1s will demolish a plate of fish and chips with gusto (or at least, that's the way it appears to the kids they attach themselves to), Type 2s will usually excuse themselves from the table before dinner is served. At best, they may nibble on a light snack in front of their experient, but you won't find them standing in the queue at a buffet. As Paul explained: 'I do not recall ever having to set a place at the table for them; they were always around, but just out of sight.'

Paul adds the following recollections to his account:

> I remember talking to them when I was alone, and I
> recall they came with me on family outings. My feelings
> towards these two 'friends' must have been strong,
> because my mum remembers a family outing that was
> nearly ruined because I had left them on the doorstep of
> the house; we had to go back for them!

Intriguingly, once again we have a QCC being 'lost'; this time by the experient himself.

Further circumstantial evidence that the QCCs were of the Type 2 species can be gleaned from Paul's description of them:

> If I had to describe them now, beyond their size and the
> colour of their clothing, I would say that they were
> elfish, with very elfish-type dress. They wore old-
> fashioned britches, long tailed jackets and stockings.

To be fair, however, Paul admits that 'this description may well be a product of my adult mind fitting them [the QCCs] into a convenient pigeonhole.'

Paul Dale has no recollection of how or when his QCCs left him, or whether in some way he metaphorically left them. He, like others, sees his QCC experience as a positive one:

> I have never viewed having these 'friends' as a bad
> thing, despite the obvious ridicule I receive at family
> gatherings when someone asks me if I've brought them
> with me.

Nevertheless, Paul knows whereof he speaks, and told me that he'd recently seen a TV documentary about a pair of twins who actually shared a QCC named Noodles. There's a thought; how do QCCs apportion themselves out in the case of twins? Time-share quasi-corporeal companions? Who knows?

Chapter twenty-five
Trigger fingered

Sian van Praagh – I love that name, it just has a ring to it – had an 'imaginary friend' called Trigger, and she wrote to me after reading my *Fortean Times* appeal for information.

Could this Trigger really be the reincarnation of Roy Rodgers' faithful steed, who starred in nearly two hundred Westerns and TV shows between 1938 and 1959? Alas, nay. Trigger, the wheeling-dealing road-sweeper of *Only Fools and Horses* fame, then? Again, nay. Sian's Trigger was seemingly a Type 4 Sage who first appeared when she was two-and-a-half years old, and stayed with her till she was approximately double that age.

Sian is quick to point out, quite correctly, that her QCC Trigger arrived on the scene 'before the *Only Fools and Horses* series, so it wouldn't be a name I would know'. It's just possible that she could have subconsciously picked it up by watching *Sunset in the West, Eyes of Texas, Apache Rose*, or some other Roy Rodgers film, but it's not really important. As Type 4 Sages often have bizarre names anyway, a human-like QCC called after a Hollywood horse is par for the course.

In some respects, as we shall see, Trigger behaved like a Type 1 QCC, but he was different in one vital respect: he was an adult, not a child. Sian seems to remember little about Trigger's physical appearance, other than that he sported a head of striking ginger hair. Unlike some Type 4 Sages, however, who have a certain insubstantial quality to them, Trigger looked perfectly solid. 'I could picture him as if he was a real person', Sian recalls.

Trigger quickly established himself as Sian's closest companion:

> According to my parents, Trigger went everywhere with me. My mum would say, 'Where's Trigger?' and I'd point and say, 'There!'

Type 4 Sages are picky eaters; or at least, like Type 2 Elementals, they're picky about who they eat with. Not so Trigger. Like Type 1

QCCs, he was happy to dine with Sian's family when the opportunity presented itself. 'Occasionally I'd make my mum set a plate out for him while we had dinner, or if I was given something I'd ask if Trigger could have one too.'

Many QCC experients have real problems when trying to recall what their quasi-corporeal pals tell them in conversation. They will happily divulge the fact that they talk to their QCC, but have problems recalling just what they talk about, or what was actually said. Trigger was somewhat different.

> My mum says that I would talk about him constantly, telling her things we'd done together. Now, when I ask her, she says that I literally did everything with him. I'd play with him, talk to him, draw with him, etc.

> My younger brother was born when I was three-years-old, and I started to talk less about Trigger, but he was still around. When my mum noticed that I hadn't spoken about him for a while she asked me where he was and I replied quite matter-of-factly, 'He's gone to Africa to help the children.' As far as I can remember, that was the last I spoke about him.

One of the puzzling factors of the QCC phenomenon is that experients often forget about their quasi-corporeal companions completely until their memory is jogged, sometimes years later. It is as if their memories are erased with great efficiency, and only resurface when someone says something like, 'Hey, can you remember that imaginary friend you used to have when you were a child?' Then, the memories will come flooding back in glorious colour and in the most vivid detail. This, I have noticed, is a particularly common facet of the Type 4 Sage experience. This is certainly what happened with Sian:

> To be honest, I'd completely forgotten all about Trigger until about six years ago. My mum asked me if I remembered Trigger, and although I'd forgotten him until then I was able to picture him. He was ginger – that I can remember – and he was an adult. My mum has always been surprised that I didn't imagine my imaginary friend to be a child.

This latter statement is particularly interesting, for it portrays how prevalent the stereotypical view of QCCs is among adults. The vast majority of grown-ups – even those who have had non-Type 1 QCCs themselves – still believe that the 'imaginary friend' phenomenon is restricted to the appearance of fictional entities who look and act like children themselves.

Alan Brookes, from Nova Scotia, told me that he had a QCC called Brad when he was a child. Brad was a conventional Type 1 companion who 'looked like a normal kid.' Alan told me that he had also sometimes been visited by a 'weird thing' that looked like a goblin. Tellingly, however, Alan only thought of Brad as a true 'imaginary friend'. The goblin, he seemed to think, had been something else entirely.

Regardless, Sian's QCC was very real to her, and even her mother seems to have considered the idea that Trigger may have been something more than a figment of her daughter's imagination: 'Thinking about it now, I recall him as a real person, which makes my mum and I wonder if he was actually an angel or spirit guide.'

Chapter twenty-six

Look, its muscle-ingesting super rabbit!

'The world is not just stranger than we know; it is stranger than we can know.' So said Heraclitus. Or Terrence McKenna, Sir Arthur Eddington, Arthur Conan Doyle, J. B. S. Haldane or perhaps even Uncle Tom Cobley, depending on which Big Book of Quotations you trust.

It's true, however. I suppose more delicate souls, not used to the cut and thrust of fortean questing, may see quasi-corporeal companions as stranger than just about anything else they've come across. Truth to tell, though, even within the bizarre world of the QCC there are varying degrees of strangeosity. (Yes, that's a made-up word but I have a very good reason for using it.*)

Tony van der Sluijs is a linguist and archaeo-astronomer. He hails from the Netherlands, has lived in both Britain and Canada, and currently resides in Seoul, South Korea. He's seen something of the world, then, and is certainly well-educated. Tony's academic background has put him in a very good position to cast a trained eye over such a curious phenomenon, even though he didn't get his degree in QCC studies. What impressed me most about Tony was the fact that, despite his background in the academic world, he was quite happy to relate to me his own QCC encounter. I have to say that it is one of the most fascinating I've come across.

Tony's case is unusual in that, as with the twins mentioned briefly in chapter twenty three, he shared his QCC with his younger brother.

According to Tony, the memories of his QCC are 'vivid, and seem accurate since I haven't dwelt much on the subject since my teenage years.'

> Roughly between the ages of four and eleven, my
> brother – one year younger than me – and I often
> engaged in a kind of play involving the appearance of a

* I like it.

heroic companion invisible to everyone except the two of us. His Dutch name was 'Ome Konijntje', which translates as 'Uncle Rabbit'.

Upon checking with my brother yesterday, I found that he had always envisioned this character as a large rabbit, possibly originally inspired by a cartoon, but I am adamant that – despite the name – I had never imagined it to be anything other than an anthropomorphic being; slightly larger than average people, with superhuman strength that he somehow acquired by consuming ball-shaped masses of energy that I at the time – in the absence of anatomical knowledge – interpreted as an 'ingestion of muscles'.

Uncle Rabbit inhabited a vast palace-like dwelling shaped like a gilded stepped pyramid or cone, a form that some might retrospectively associate with the archetypal 'golden mountain' of world mythology.

The numerous adventures at the side of Uncle Rabbit are all but forgotten, and all I remember now is that I once drew a map with significant locations relating to the stories. Crucial to the story is the extent to which we believed in the physical reality of Uncle Rabbit; a question I had never asked myself until yesterday.

When asked, my brother was fairly confident that he had always known that all this was just fiction and had just allowed himself at times to become immersed in this fantasy world. As far as the later years are concerned, my own memories would underpin this impression, but to the best of my knowledge I cannot guarantee that this also applied to the earliest period, before I could even read. It may well be that Uncle Rabbit had originally appeared to us as genuine, rather than just a fantasy friend.

The plays invariably involved the two of us jumping and leaping across the room – or outside – like mad; a type of behaviour that may – with the benefit of hindsight – have been conducive to the most active imagination or 'tuning' into the story that was being woven.

Quite – but whatever the truth, the fact is that Tony and his brother both enjoyed the company of a quasi-corporeal companion that was (a) either a human or a rabbit, and (b) sustained him/itself by ingesting spherical balls of energy.

It's hard to classify just what type of QCC Tony had, then. Uncle Rabbit may have been a Type 3 Animal, or perhaps a Type 4 Sage. We do not need to know. To understand the true nature of the phenomenon we need to savour the presence of the QCC, not clinically dissect it.

Chapter twenty-seven

A place for everything and everything in its place

Taxonomy is a scientific term derived from two Greek words; *taxis*, meaning 'to separate' and *nomos*, meaning 'law'. Taxonomy, then, is the process of dividing things up and placing them into a logical framework by some sensible system of classification. Carl Linnaeus, the famous eighteenth century Swedish scientist, was largely responsible for creating the system of classifying living things that is still in use today. Such systems are generally known as taxonomies.

Creating a taxonomy is not always easy, for one must first decide what criteria one wishes to use. By way of example, suppose that I had in my possession two objects, a red ball and a blue cube. I may decide to classify the objects by colour, or perhaps shape. As both objects have a different colour and a different shape, they will undoubtedly hold different positions in my taxonomy. On the other hand, suppose that both the ball and the cube were red in colour. If I decide not to use shape as a classification criterion, then they may both end up in the same position in my taxonomy classed as 'Objects, red'. The fact that both objects have different shapes does not matter, for shape is not a relevant criterion in my classification system.

In this book I have essentially created a taxonomy in which a number of criteria play a role in deciding where each QCC sits. These criteria include, but are not limited to, appearance, behaviour, environment, duration and similarity.

Importantly I make no claims that any one type of QCC is related to any other biologically, chemically or in any other way. Similarity does not always imply relationship. A frog may be green and a sprig of mint may be green. This gives them both a superficial similarity to each other, but does not imply that they are related in any meaningful way, other than that they are both 'living things'. Nevertheless, if colour was the only criterion in my taxonomical system of classification, I would actually be creating a close 'relationship' between them, although such a relationship would probably be of little value.

During my research, it became clear to me that QCCs usually fall into one of four distinct categories, and that one of those categories had two distinct sub-types. In the case of Type 4 Wackies, the two sub-types – Sages and Animates – have been grouped together because the differences between them were, to me, much more subtle than the differences between the other types. The similarities were also, to me, somewhat stronger. This taxonomy is not set in stone, however, and I do not claim that it is the only workable one. Research into this field is still in its infancy. Further, the taxonomy I have employed is used equally as much to help the author as it is the reader.

What, then, makes an entity a quasi-corporeal companion? There are a number of common denominators, but few are shared by every type. As a general rule, QCCs can be identified by some (but never all) of the following criteria:

- They are entities which seem to possess sentience.

- They have the ability to appear and disappear at will.

- They will appear as young children.

- They will appear as animals.

- They will appear as 'elementals'.

- They will appear as adult humans who dress in a ways that emphasise a cultural background of sorts.

- They will appear as animated objects.

- They will only appear to one experient, who will almost always be a young child.

- They will be reluctant to discuss where they come from or give other personal details about themselves to the experient.

- They will possess a conventional name.

- They will possess a name which has a superficial appearance of conventionality.

- They will possess a name which is a 'double-barrelled repetitive'.

- They will have a strong disposition towards giving advice and counsel to the experient.

- They will leave strange 'gifts' for the experient and/or the experient's family.

The study of quasi-corporeal companions – or whatever one may wish to call them – is still in its infancy. I expect – nay, hope – that further research may produce better methods of classification. For now, however, I merely hope to have provided a system that will allow experients and researchers alike to classify QCCs provisionally and give a little clarity to a field of research that is still largely virgin territory.

Chapter twenty-eight

Witch imaginary friend was that?

Diana Jarvis is the editor of *Vision* magazine, one of the country's leading journals dealing with spiritual, holistic and paranormal matters. Diana is well versed, then, in matters which do not fall within the normal scope of daily life. While other, more conventional souls are wondering whether to purchase de-caf or regular, Diana will probably be poring over an article on Inuit spirituality or a feature about how to invigorate your chakras. It's a tough job, but somebody has to do it.

Between birth and the age of five, Diana confesses to having been 'a very lonely and insular child.' She spent a lot of her time either reading books or out in the garden watching the butterflies. However, she also interacted on a regular basis with a QCC – probably a Type 2 Elemental, although we can't be certain – whom she simply called The Witch. Diana's QCC also bears some resemblance to a Type 4 Sage.

From the outset, what I found intriguing about Diana's account was her profession that, 'I never saw her, either in my imagination or in reality. She was simply there to bargain with, as a 'presence'.' On a number of occasions I came across experients who told a similar tale; they had a QCC whom they could not see, and yet they were fully aware of its presence.

Almost all Type 4 Sages can be seen, and they normally present themselves as a stereotype of a culture different to that in which the experient lives. Those that cannot be seen, I have noticed, often have an epithet that is descriptive of their nature. In fact, the epithet will give the experient a clue as to what the QCC would look like if it *could* be seen. Diana's invisible companion was called The Witch, a title which would have allowed her at least to visualise a stereotypical witch even though she could not see the 'real' QCC that had befriended her.

Diana told me that The Witch, 'was not unkind, but if I wanted something for myself or for others, I had to make a deal with her. I usually offered to pass some kind of simple test (such as finding a green acorn before 3 p.m.) in order to obtain said item.'

Barry Colson*, from Adelaide, told me a similar story:

> My friend was a bit like a gnome. He'd help me out whenever I needed it, but he never made life easy. Before he'd do whatever I wanted him to do, he'd ask me to bring him something. One time he asked me to bring him a match box filled with a mixture of tea and coffee. On another occasion he wanted strips of newspaper. Everything he ever asked for just seemed like so much rubbish. I couldn't figure it out. The strange thing was that he would get very excited when I brought him what he wanted. He'd jump up and down, as if you'd given him a handful of dollars.
>
> He used to have a bag attached to his belt. Everything I ever gave him went in that bag. God knows what he did with it all when he went back to wherever he came from.
>
> But you know, he never once let me down. If I asked him for a favour, he'd do it – providing I wasn't being greedy or asking him for something unreasonable.

Perhaps these QCCs make the granting of wishes conditional to teach their young charges a lesson; that good things come at a price, and that there's no such thing as a free lunch.

Diana had a good relationship with her QCC, which, if it was a Type 2 Elemental, was pretty chatty. 'I would talk to her a lot and was occasionally reprimanded at the family dinner table for talking to myself.' I know the feeling. However, Diana later explained that when she 'talked' to The Witch the conversation did not take the form of conventional dialogue: 'It wasn't 'words', if you understand what I mean. I would just think an idea, and I'd know what she was thinking.'

Diana seems to have adopted a policy of not discussing The Witch with her family as a matter of course.

> The only time The Witch was ever mentioned to my family was when a ball-bearing inexplicably found its way into my nose. I remember that I was very young, because the doctor in the hospital that removed it was

Diana Jarvis

black, and it was the first time I'd seen a black person anywhere but on television. I said that The Witch had put it there. I wasn't the sort of child to blame anyone else for what I'd done (there *was* no one else!), so it was out of character for me to do this. I was also pretty bright and knew that I was the only one that spoke to The Witch and so no one would believe me about her anyway. I still don't know why I said that she had done it.

This was seemingly one of the few occasions in my research when an experient acknowledged trying to blame their QCC for something they hadn't done, so I solicited Diana for some more detail. What she told me was interesting.

First, I asked Diana whether The Witch did or did not insert the ball bearing into her nasal cavity. On reflection, she told me that she genuinely couldn't remember. It just possibly may have been The Witch, or it may have been Diana herself. This leaves a question mark hanging over the issue of whether The Witch really was the victim of a miscarriage of justice or not.

Next, I wanted to know whether there had been any repercussions from The Witch after Diana had – rightly or wrongly – accused her of putting the ball bearing up her nose: 'No, definitely not. She was very kind and never berated or criticised me for anything. In fact, I don't ever remember discussing the issue with her after that.'

Not unnaturally, Diana has some quite developed notions about the nature of QCCs. As the editor of a magazine that deals with such matters on a monthly basis, one could hardly expect anything else: 'I have always believed that The Witch was an extension of my imagination (which was usually pretty fertile) or my Higher Self.'

I probed Diana a little more deeply on this point, and she related something that I'd never heard from a QCC experient before:

> The Witch seemed to occupy a place within my head.
> She was inside of me, and I knew where. The weird
> thing was that although I say 'inside' my head, I felt that
> she was actually outside of it in some way. I had a very
> strong feeling that she was present approximately four
> feet to the left of my head, and slightly in front of me.

Despite the fact that Diana genuinely believes that The Witch was in some way an extension of her imagination – or even her own personality, perhaps – she admits candidly that there are some incongruities connected to this idea.

> I really don't know why I called her The Witch, or even
> why she seemed that way to me. There was no history
> of witchcraft in my family, and I had no interest in the
> subject myself; couldn't have, given my solitude and
> young age.

Perhaps, then, The Witch may have enjoyed a more objective reality than at first imagined.

Diana Jarvis has had a hard life in many respects. She is a survivor who has battled through tough times and built a successful career for herself. Intriguingly, she suspects that The Witch may have helped her in this regard.

> Around twenty years later I became a solitary Wiccan
> and also represented the Pagan Federation in my local
> area. One of my proudest achievements to date is
> getting together a chaplain from the Church of England
> and a High Priestess from the Craft in a mutual spirit of
> religious tolerance and understanding.

Did this character, 'The Witch', know that I would need to be understanding of other faiths when I got older? Or what job I would eventually do?

Good questions deserving of answers. Diana is not the only experient to hint that their QCC may have subtly prepared them for responsibilities they would come to shoulder in later life.

Elsie Green, a sales representative from North Yorkshire, told me that her QCC, a Type 3 Animal (a mouse called Bon), used to play games with her in which Elsie always had to pretend to try and sell the mouse something.

> Sometimes she would just shake her head and pretend not to be interested in buying my sweets, or whatever I was trying to sell her. She'd just squeak, 'Try harder! Try harder!'
>
> I honestly think that Bon taught me how to be a good salesperson. If it wasn't for the lessons I learnt then, I don't think I'd be doing the job I'm doing now.

Undeniably Diana's explanation for the QCC phenomenon – at least in her own case – may be correct. Perhaps the Witch was just an extension of her own self. This lends itself to yet another question: just where do QCCs live?

Chapter twenty-nine

Honestly, it's like talking to a brick wall

Karen Miller, a catering manager from Gateshead, had a number of QCCs as a child. Almost certainly they were Type 2 Elementals, but there are some peculiarities about her case that demand scrutiny.

Most Type 2 QCCs live outdoors, but occasionally they seem to dwell within the house of the experient.

Gef the talking mongoose (a Type 3 Animal) and Ebert the Skeleton (a Type 4 Animate) also lived indoors, and the reader will recall that they inhabited the strangest of places. Gef lived in the attic, although he would occasionally venture into wall cavities. Ebert lived in a radiator. Karen's QCCs also lived in a wall, but more of that later.

There is a common denominator between all interior-dwelling QCCs apart from Type 4 Animates; they seem to specifically choose living accommodation in places where the residents of the house cannot see them: the attic, a cavity wall, under the carpet, etc. As far as I can see there are two obvious possibilities; interior-dwelling QCCs choose to live in such places either because they feel comfortable there, or because they are places in which they can hide and keep out of the sight of residents without too much bother. Rats and mice do not as a rule nest in the middle of the lounge or on top of the TV set. They will live behind cupboards or in the loft, where they are safe from an angry householder wielding a shovel.

Type 4 Animates do not need to engage in such subterfuge, for when they are not animated and presenting themselves as quasi-corporeal companions they usually appear as everyday household objects.

But there is a third, less obvious possibility. What if the place they reside in, inside the dwelling, appears markedly different to the QCC than it does to the experient? What if there is a whole world – a different dimension, even – behind that wall, radiator or bath panel that we humans cannot see?

In 1950, the writer C.S. Lewis penned a book which would come to capture the hearts and minds of children, as well as adults, the world over. *The Lion, the Witch and the Wardrobe* was the first volume in *The Chronicles of Narnia* series, although later a prequel was written entitled *The Magician's Nephew*. The prequel was eventually marketed as book one, thus making *The Lion, the Witch and the Wardrobe* book two, at least chronologically speaking.

The plot concerns four children who, during the Second World War, are evacuated from London and send to live with an elderly academic out in the sticks. His house is large and rambling – a veritable adventure playground for four inquisitive youngsters.

To cut a long story extremely short, one of the children – Lucy – takes it upon herself to clamber inside an old wardrobe. Now this wardrobe is not *any* old wardrobe, no sir; it is actually a gateway or portal to another world, the mystical kingdom of Narnia. The rest of the book, as you might guess, concerns the adventures of the four children in this other world.

There are two facts about the Kingdom of Narnia that need to be drawn to the attention of the reader. Firstly, the entire world of Narnia seems to exist within – or just beyond – the confines of the wardrobe. Secondly, those who enter it may stay for hours or even days, but when they return to the 'real' world they find that no time seems to have passed at all during the interval.

The idea that there may be portals in our world that lead to other worlds or alternative realities is a fascinating one, and a number of science fiction series on TV have exploited the theme extremely successfully; *Stargate* is probably the best example.

In January 2000 popular music fans and sci-fi buffs alike were enthralled by the release of the latest Aqua single, *Cartoon Heroes*. Both the lyrics and the excellent accompanying video captured perfectly a bygone age – the mid-Thirties to the early Sixties – when pulp science fiction had its own distinctive character. *Dan Dare, War of the Worlds, The Twilight Zone* and *The Outer Limits* – we'll never see their like again, and we are the less for their passing. One of the most popular themes with early science fiction writers was that of alternate dimensions; twilight realms which housed all manner of strange creatures and dastardly space villains. 'B' movies like *The Creature from the Fifth Dimension* and awful novels such as *They Came from Dimension Ten* may not have been award-winning stuff, but they thrilled legions of bored citizens who had few other means of indulging their desire for absolute escapism.

But could there really be other dimensions – perhaps entire universes – which exist alongside our own? Is it possible that 'other realities' really exist, strange worlds on another plane of which we are entirely ignorant? In recent years, advances in quantum physics theory have demonstrated that our world, and the universe as a whole, is a far stranger place than we ever gave it credit for. We now know that time, for instance, does not really flow in the simple 'past/present/future' linear stream that we always imagined, and that matter can be made to react in bizarre ways which almost defy logic under certain conditions. Currently accepted models of the universe include six or more dimensions. Because the 'physical reality' of the dimensions we cannot directly experience may be entirely different from ours, our dimensions and these others may actually be in the same geographical location, but operating on a different 'wavelength', so to speak. It is strange to think that there may be other worlds existing alongside our own which we simply cannot touch, hear nor see.

A correspondent once told me of a strange experience he had when he was a young boy of ten. He was sitting in the back garden of his home in the Primrose area of Jarrow, Tyne and Wear. It was a beautiful summer's day and the sun was shining brightly.

At the top of the back garden stood a trellis and an archway covered in ivy and other climbing plants. Suddenly, the trellis arch began to shimmer 'like heat coming off a hot road.' Then the shimmering stopped, and he was astonished to see that the view through the archway had changed completely. Instead of houses across the road, he could see rolling hills and forests.

> I was shocked, as you can imagine. I could see trees,
> but they were strange trees like none I'd ever seen
> before or seen after. They were like palm trees, but they
> had large orange globes stuck to the trunk in a circle
> about eighteen inches from the ground. In fact, all the
> plants seemed strange.

This strange vision only lasted for about fifteen seconds. Then the archway shimmered again and everything went back to normal. The witness swears that this strange experience really occurred. Although he was frightened, he never told his parents. 'They were not the understanding sort', he confided. He was also careful to avoid going through that arch again, frightened that 'something might happen' and he would never come back.

Was this simply a vision of the remote past? A glimpse of how this area once appeared in primeval times? Or did this youngster catch sight of another dimension entirely, one which holds unseen wonders and opportunities, if only we could find a way to explore it?

Tom Jadz, who also lived in Jarrow, told me a fascinating story about a dream he had which reoccurred over and over for a period of several months. In fact, the dream was so intense that Tom is convinced it wasn't really a dream at all, but rather a vision of the future.

> Usually it would start in the same way. I'd be in a spacesuit, peering out through the visor, with air being pumped into the suit from a unit in my backpack, but it was extremely hot and clammy. In front of me would be a vast landscape of red rocks and mountains. I knew I was on Mars.

> Just to my left and slightly behind me was another astronaut. I remember him talking to me. On one occasion he said, 'Come on – you know how easy they get stirred up after dark. The folks down below will go ape if we have to use the HIL, and we can't white-light them in case someone sees us.

> The last thing I remember is quickly walking back to the living module feeling very apprehensive.

Tom says that during these visions 'everything made sense', but after waking he hadn't a clue what much of it meant. Who were 'they' that got 'stirred up after dark'? What was an 'HIL', and how on earth do you 'white-light' someone or something?

On another occasion, Tom remembers having a conversation with a NASA official over the radio. 'He was called George, and he was alarmed. I remember him shouting, "Evac! Evac! Get that line out of there and shut that thing down before they see it!" What it all meant I don't know, although I think I did know what it meant when I was actually in the dream.'

If Tom wasn't dreaming, could he have had a chilling premonition of man's first trip to the Red Planet? If so, it seems that we weren't exactly welcome there.

Interestingly, premonitions of this sort – if indeed they are premonitions – can sometimes be tested. We know that the USA plans to send a manned expedition to Mars within the next two decades. Could there be a 'George' already working for NASA on the Mars project? Do the terms 'HIL', 'white-light' and 'Evac' mean anything in astronautical parlance? If so, then Tom's dream may have some credibility.

Tom says that the dreams stopped as suddenly as they started. He has no idea what they meant, but he is convinced that they were 'real'; that is, not something dreamed up by an overactive imagination. 'I only wish I could have retained the knowledge I had when I was actually dreaming', he said, 'but it never happened. During my dreams I was an astronaut. I understood the terminology used and everything. But, when I woke up, it would just fade away.'

Of course, what Tom experienced may not have been a glimpse into another dimension, but simply a peek at a small slice of mankind's future. However, what the experience does illustrate that, in an altered state of consciousness, such alternate dimensions may only be a hair's breadth away.

Most readers will have seen those wonderful old black-and-white re-runs of the aforementioned *The Outer Limits* and *The Twilight Zone* on TV. Some may even remember those equally wonderful comic books – also in black-and-white – with epithets such as *Creepy Worlds, Weird Tales* and *Astounding Stories.* Back in the 1960s, no self-respecting science fiction story or movie failed to make mention of that mysterious netherworld known as the Fourth Dimension. The Fourth Dimension was, according to popular wisdom, the home of flying saucers, the repository of fairies and the happy hunting ground of the Loch Ness monster to boot.

We live in a three-dimensional world. We think of things, and formulate our perspective of them, in terms of width, height and depth. If there is indeed a fourth dimension, then, it is unlikely to be a 'place', but rather another means of quantifying things of which we are currently unaware.

Because of this, philosophers now prefer to talk not about 'other dimensions', but rather of 'alternate realities' – other worlds which may be parallel to our own, but invisible to us.

If such worlds exist, what might they be like? The short answer is that we do not know, because the laws of physics which govern our world may not apply in others. We may find that the 'Fourth Dimension', if it exists, is an alien landscape not unlike those seen on sci-fi 'B' movies decades ago. It may be teeming with alien life forms, or, alternatively, a barren wilderness similar to the surface of Mars or Pluto.

Over the years there have been thousands of mysterious disappearances recorded. Men, women and children of all ages and backgrounds have, quite literally, vanished from the face of the earth. Could these people have accidentally wandered through a portal of some kind, a doorway into an 'alternate reality' similar to the Narnia immortalised by C.S. Lewis? Did this doorway then close, trapping them there forever?

There is an old Jewish legend about a man who falls asleep in a cave while picking figs. He wakes up and, finding that it is getting dark, makes his way home. On his arrival he is astonished to find a stranger living in his house. He protests, only to be told that everyone he knew had died decades previously. It was as if he had been in a state of suspended animation for years, or at least living in a place where the flow of time was slower. In his basket the bewildered man still had branches of fresh figs. This convinced the other man that he was telling the truth, because the fig-picking season had finished months previously.

Where had he been all those years? Narnia, perhaps.

In 2002, I was hosting the launch of one of my books when I met George Ross and Salvador Parcon, two sailors who hail from the chilly climes of Nova Scotia, Canada. I spent some time talking to George and Salvador, and found that, like all mariners, they had several good stories to tell. I promised to mention them in my *Bizarre* column, and in the same article related two tales from their homeland.

The first concerns a sailor from France who, many moons ago, was dropped off on the L'île à Frisée near beautiful Nova Scotia by his colleagues. For whatever reason they decided to stay aboard the ship which was anchored off-shore, perhaps wary of the biting wind which can chill you to the bone. He decided to explore the place, and traipsed for some distance over the barren, windswept isle.

You have to visit Nova Scotia to appreciate how lonely one can feel on the myriad islands and rocky outcrops which litter the coast. The small populace, biting wind and crashing waves only add to the feeling that Mother Nature really is in charge here.

The Nova Scotians are hardened to the climate, but ironically it is the inhospitable climate itself which makes our story all the more difficult to understand. According to legend, the young sea-dog eventually stumbled across a beautiful garden filled with exotic flowers which exuded the most beautiful fragrances. In contrast with the rest of the island it seemed like paradise. Birds with fancy plumes flew through the air, which – unlike that outside the garden – was warm and invigorating. For some time he wandered around the garden, overcome with its breathtaking beauty and diversity of flora and fauna. Mystified as to how such a tropical beauty spot could thrive in such an inhospitable climate, he decided to get his friends to take a look.

The sailor made his way back to the shore, carefully picking his way between the boulders and rocks. Eventually he saw the ship at anchor, and shouted as loud as he could. At some point a boat was lowered, and several sailors rowed ashore to see what all the fuss was about. 'Wait till you see what I've found!' he exclaimed. 'You've never seen anything like it!'

The man turned and retraced his steps, his curious colleagues following closely behind. At long last they turned a corner, and the sailor's jaw dropped in amazement. The garden had gone, all trace of it erased. It was as if it had never existed. In its place was the same wilderness that covered the rest of the island. The mystery was never solved.

The second story concerns another Nova Scotian folk tale which is also set just off the coast.

Off the eastern coast of Nova Scotia lies a small rock called Duck Island. One day, many years ago, two friends decided to go for a stroll across its barren surface. As they walked along the coast they found, to their horror, a human leg bone lying there. The stunned pair looked around but could see no other body parts, clothing or artefacts which could shed any light on the mystery. Several things puzzled the walkers. Who could it belong to? What was it doing there, and why had it not been found before? More to the point, what should be done with it now?

The pair had brought a packed lunch with them, and so they moved to a respectful distance before eating it. The sight of a human thigh-bone can be a mite off-putting when you're tucking into a luncheon meat sandwich.

Eventually they reached a decision – they would bury the bone with due solemnity and dignity. However, when they walked back to the place where they'd found it, they were astonished to see that it had completely disappeared. More puzzled than ever, they began to search. Every square inch of ground was scoured, but no sign of their grim discovery could now be found.

Who took the bone? The tide was apparently too far out to have carried it into the sea, there were no other humans on the island and a bird big enough to pinch it would have been immediately visible to the hikers. In fact, the isle was devoid of any birds or animals which could have done such a thing.

Mysteries like this are hard to fathom. It is tempting to suggest that there must be a logical explanation for what happened, and indeed there very well may be. On the other hand, we cannot rule out the possibility that something paranormal was at work.

Maybe the two hikers hallucinated – but if so, would they have both seen the same thing? Highly unlikely. Perhaps they saw a ghostly image or apparition of some kind. Had the thigh-bone lain upon the beach hundreds or even thousands of years ago, only to leap through time and appear momentarily in the twentieth century?

Strange appearances and disappearances such as this are not as uncommon as one might think. Curiously, they often take place in remote 'wilderness' areas far away from civilisation. What happens when we visit such places? Could it be that, as the modern world in which we live fades into the distance, the past finds it easier to resurface?

Some years ago, a national magazine carried a letter from a reader which detailed a very strange experience indeed. The reader's friend had got lost in a park on her way to an appointment, and turned up twenty minutes late in a rather distressed state. There is nothing inherently strange about this, except that the park was only one quarter of a mile long and one eighth of a mile wide. How can someone become lost in such a small area, particularly one they are familiar with? Quite easily, it seems.

Cases like that above are not rare. I investigated one myself two years ago, in which a man said he could not find his way out of a long street of shops. No matter which direction he went in, he kept finding himself back in the middle facing the other way. It's easy to laugh at stories like this, but the chap was genuinely traumatised by his experience. 'I started to sweat and my heart was pounding. I wasn't imagining this. It was a good fifteen minutes before I reached the other end. It was just crazy. I kept walking, but the end of the street got no closer. I was in a real panic.'

There is an old legend that if you stray into the territory of 'the little people' you can become 'pixie-led'. The story goes that pixies can toy with humans by making them go round in circles. The solution, it was said, was to turn your jacket inside out. For some reason this would break the spell.

There could, of course, be more prosaic explanations. Certain illnesses can make those who suffer from them disorientated, while stress and tiredness may also play a part. However, not all cases are as easily explained away. There is a real possibility that certain conditions can allow physical principles such as time, space, matter, force and motion to become distorted. Anyone caught up in such a distortion could experience all manner of bizarre phenomena, the cases above being classic examples. Some researchers believe that such anomalies are caused when we accidentally slip, albeit temporarily, into another dimension.

And then there's the matter of Black Holes, those centres of supergravity which suck anything and everything in, before expelling the same material, in rather compressed form, out somewhere else. One theory is that Black Holes could actually be used as shortcuts to take us from one part of the universe to another in the blink of an eye. How on earth we're supposed to survive the gravitational pressure – which can condense something as big as planet earth to the size of pea – no one seems to have worked out.

Despite the logistical difficulties, a number of UFO abductees claim to have visited other planets – other solar systems, even – courtesy of extraterrestrials who have allegedly taken them there, in a flying saucer, when they had an hour or two to spare. But here's the real problem. Satellite and probe photographs have demonstrated that the bleak terrains of the planets in our solar system are nothing like the way most abductees describe them.

The moon, according to one famous 1950s UFO buff, was, at least on its dark side, covered with forests and all manner of strange flora and fauna. One nineteenth century religious leader even said that the moon was populated by eight foot-tall humans who wore top hats and lived to be a thousand years old. If true, then Neil Armstrong, Buzz Aldrin and others don't seem to have bumped into them. Mind you, if they *had* bumped into them, would they have said anything?

Seriously though, we cannot discount the possibility that life does exist on other worlds. Many ancient traditions – such as those of Native Americans – speak of 'Sky People' who came from the stars many millennia ago. If they visited us on our home world, then they must have one of their own.

Perhaps the most fascinating tales come from those who claim to have visited other worlds in their sleep. One correspondent told me that the same landscape kept appearing every time in her dreams; a hot, dry desert with pale blue sand and a purple-tinged sky. What convinced this lady that she was really travelling to this place in her sleep was the fact that, whenever she had this dream, she would wake up and find grains of sand and dust in her bed and adhering to her nightclothes. Alas, she did not keep these particles for analysis.

If science ever does find a way of travelling to other worlds quickly and easily – an almost impossible task, some would say – the potential would be beyond our imagination. Imagine what it would be like to be the first human to set foot on a planet at the other end of the galaxy, or the first person to dive into an ocean on a world thousands of light years away. We can but wonder.

Having demonstrated how close we may unwittingly be to worlds or dimensions beyond our ken, we may now return to the tale related by Karen Miller. From the age of two, Karen became aware that there were people – of sorts – living behind the walls in her home. Karen would talk to them when she was upset, and they would help her. The entities who lived behind the walls looked like 'sprites or elves,' Karen said. They were young, both 'boys and girls,' although there was little to differentiate the two sexes. According to Karen they both much pretty much alike, and had an almost hermaphroditic quality. They were short, and had 'windswept, spiky hair' that stuck upright as if it had been severely gelled. Their clothing was 'gossamer-like,' and both translucent and insubstantial.

As with most multiple Type 2 Elemental appearances, there was one entity who always 'took the lead'. A male, he always appeared before the rest. In fact, Karen noticed that it was *always* the males who

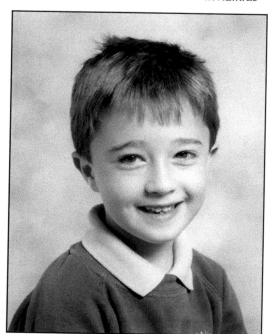

Jared Hallowell

appeared first. Sometimes, only one QCC would appear. Sometimes it would be two or more, but Karen distinctly recalls that on a number of occasions she was visited by up to thirty QCCs simultaneously.

Karen's distinct impression was that the entities lived in a 'kingdom' behind the walls of her home. They were not so much living *in* the walls as stepping from their own world into ours *through* the walls. There is, as you can see, an uncanny parallel here between Karen's experience and the tale told by C.S. Lewis in *The Lion, the Witch and the Wardrobe*. Whenever Karen's QCCs would appear through the wall – it could be any wall in the house, although they seemed to prefer one particular bedroom – something seemed to prevent them disengaging themselves from it completely. Part of their body – an arm, a leg, their lower torso, or whatever – would remain 'in' the wall, as if it was important to them not to lose contact with it completely. If Karen's experience has any degree of objective reality, then the question arises as to why her QCCs seemed to find continual contact with the wall they were emanating from so important. Could it be that if such contact was severed completely they may have experienced difficulty in returning to their own world or dimension?

Lulie and Thomas as drawn by Jared

Karen's QCCs stopped appearing to her when she was approximately three-and-a-half years of age. Her recollections are now scant, but she remembers that her QCCs would always fix problems for her when she was troubled.

Karen's nephew, Jared, had two Type 1s QCCs called Thomas and Lulie. As per usual with QCCs of this type, they never appeared together. Like his aunt Karen, Jared has virtually no recollections of how he interacted with Thomas and Lulie, even though he is currently just six years of age. He does remember that Thomas dressed in a 'strange' manner and wore something like a dressing gown, except that 'it wasn't a dressing gown, really.' Lulie dressed completely conventionally.

Jared recalls asking his QCCs where they came from, but they could never tell him – or refused, perhaps. They would play with him until he went to sleep, and then they'd go off and 'do their own thing.' According to Jared, they never needed to sleep themselves…

Chapter thirty

Grip Yodel and the magic doorstop

Grip Yodel was the Type 1 QCC of Bernie McKay, who read my letter in the *Fortean Times*. According to Bernie, Grip had a 'magic doorstop' with which he performed all sorts of tricks. The doorstop was made of brass, and was shaped like a milk bottle. 'You could even see the outline of the tinfoil top,' Bernie told me. 'It looked like a conventional milk bottle in every sense, but it was made of solid brass.'

I asked Bernie how he knew it was a doorstop. 'Because he told me it was,' he replied. 'Grip said that he used the doorstop to prop open the gate to his cottage, but he could do magic with it by waving it around his head and shouting, 'Wahoo!''

Of course.

Grip Yodel dressed as conventionally as his name, which was not very. He wore a big, red hat and a blue suit:

> The suit was quite tattered. It had patches on it which I think covered holes, and looked incredibly worn. I remember asking him if he wanted me to get my mother to sew him a new one on her sewing machine, but he declined. He said that if he tried to take anything back from this world to his it would just disappear.

> There was another funny thing about Grip. He always appeared by the back door which led into the garden, and there was a rope tied around his ankle which disappeared under a large stone which we used to scrape the mud off our boots. Grip would never venture father than the rope would stretch. It was as if he had to be attached to the stone, for some reason.

One can't help wonder whether there is a parallel between this aspect of Bernie's story and the account given by Karen Miller, in which her QCCs seemingly could not detach themselves completely from the walls they appeared through.

On one occasion, Grip wanted to know why I wasn't at school. I told him it was because the heating system had broken down. He waved the magic doorstop around his head, shouted 'Wahoo!' as usual and then disappeared.

At first I thought he had fixed the heating at my school, but he hadn't. Just then, my mother shouted me inside and gave me a big bar of chocolate she'd just found. I swear that Grip Yodel put it there.

Chapter thirty-one
What's it all about, Alfie?

Alfie was the QCC of Jean Barry*. Jean contacted me after reading my article in *Cosmic Connections*, and wanted to tell me her story. Unlike most correspondents, Jean – a freelance writer – went into copious detail about her experiences and believes that she may actually have visited the world from whence her Type 1 QCC came. As no other correspondent had ever made such a claim, I was intrigued.

I have decided not to edit down Jean's story. Much of the detail may superficially seem trivial, but it is often in the seemingly trivial where important facts can be gleaned. The fascination which her story holds is not in any way jaded by its length, as you will see.

Jean was born in Staten Island, one of the five boroughs of New York City. Situated on an island of the same name, Staten Island is the least populated of the five boroughs and is often seen as the 'poor relation' of the other four.

> My schooling was pretty poor, but that was my fault. It wasn't that I didn't possess the wherewithal to succeed; I just didn't try. I suppose one could say that I was lazy. Dad wanted me to be a lawyer, Mom wanted me to go into medicine like my aunt. I ended up working in a department store owned by this nice old Jewish guy. I loved working there, but my parents found it an embarrassment.
>
> I remember one day my aunt came to visit.
>
> 'Is Jean still working at that... *place*?' she enquired.
>
> Mom knew that she was looking down her nose at us. Her own son, my cousin, was a detective and she was so proud of him. She was squirming, and the only way out of it was to tell a big, fat lie.
>
> 'Well, they're training her to be an *executive*, you know. She only works behind the counter temporarily

so that she can get some experience of what the uh…*lower* workers have to do. They say within two years she'll be right at the top.'

This was all nonsense, of course. I was never going to be an executive, and my mother knew it. She was just embarrassed because her daughter was selling cheap perfume from behind a board.

The thing that got me through was my memory of Alfie. He'd been an invisible friend of mine until I was around eight or nine, I can't remember exactly. Even though I hadn't seen him for years, sometimes I could sense his presence around me. With Alfie beside me, things would be okay.'

I asked Jean how and when Alfie had first introduced himself.

Oh! I can remember it distinctly! My grandma had taken us for the weekend, so I was away from home from Friday evening until Sunday evening. When I got home, I went to my room. The next day we were having a 'show and tell' at school, and I had to prepare. I was nervous, because it was my first one. I think I was only six years, if I remember correctly, and I had to 'show and tell' about my favourite doll.

I got my doll from the closet and put a fresh dress on her. Just then, this little boy appeared by the door. I didn't know him then, but it was Alfie. I can't remember exactly what he said, but my recollection is that he wanted to help. He stayed a while and I suppose we talked.

The next day I went to school and did my 'show and tell'. I got top grade, you know! That's because I recited a rhyme:

> Lena is my favourite doll.
> She lives in the cupboard in the wall.
> She likes candy, she likes fruit.
> Lena doll is really cute.

My teacher asked me who had made the poem up. She obviously thought there was no way a kid of my age could have composed that. I think that she was even surprised I'd remembered it, considering my age.

The truth is, I don't think I did compose that rhyme. I think it must have been Alfie. I don't remember him reciting it, or helping me memorise it, but I just don't think it came out of *me*. I just don't think I could have written a rhyme like that.

One of the peculiarities about QCCs is the way that their first appearance doesn't seem to engender any feelings of alarm in the young experients. During my research I asked a number of young children what they would do if they suddenly found a little boy or girl whom they didn't know in their house. Almost all said, 'I'd run and tell my mum and dad.' The others basically said that they didn't know what they'd do, and looked puzzled. Jean, like almost every other experient I came across, just seemed to accept that the presence of their QCC was a perfectly natural event.

I asked Jean to tell me more about Alfie.

Well, he was around nine or ten years old, I would guess, and he wore short pants and a hooped woollen top with no sleeves. He had blond hair, I recall, and his shoes – they were brown – were very scuffed, as if they needed a good polish.

Jean told me that there wasn't really anything about Alfie that would make him stand out in a crowd. 'He was just an ordinary kid', she affirmed.

Jean recalls that Alfie visited her 'just about every day'. Sometimes his visits would last just a few minutes. Other times he would stay for hours. I also wanted to know whether her parents ever heard or saw anything that would have convinced them that Alfie was more than a mere figment of her imagination.

You know, that's something that's really hard to answer. When he first started to come around, my mom would come up to my room quite a lot and say, 'Jean, who are you talking to?' When I told her it was Alfie, she'd just smile and go back to the kitchen. After a while she stopped doing this, but it may have been because she'd just got used to the idea that I was talking to someone who was just part of my imagination.

There was one time when Dad had given me a large bag of potato chips. He told me not to eat them all, as I wouldn't have room for supper. I ate a few, and Alfie ate the rest. Dad was annoyed, and thought that I'd eaten them all. As a punishment I wasn't given supper, even though I was still hungry. He thought that I'd eaten them all, but I hadn't.'

Jean recalled another time when Alfie turned up with 'dirt all over his shoes', and 'bits of it got onto the carpet.'

> Mom was sure that I had been outside, but I hadn't. She said there was no other way the dirt could have gotten on to the carpet in my room. I told her that Alfie did it, but as you may guess she didn't believe me.

Although Alfie inadvertently got Jean into trouble every now and then, in every other respect he was a model companion. He never lost his temper, scolded her or did anything to cause her upset.

Like other QCCs, Alfie was remarkably coy about his place of origin:

> I asked him on a number of occasions where he came from, and the only answer I ever got was, 'Out there'. I never found out where 'out there' was. All I knew, or felt, was that it was somewhere outside my room.

Mealtimes could be fractious in the Barry household, as Jean's parents refused point blank to set a place at the table for Alfie.

> I think that if they'd set a place for him it would have been like admitting that he really existed. They couldn't go that far; but you know, there was something odd about their attitude. I don't think that they didn't believe he existed. At least… I don't think they were confident in that belief. Deep down they didn't want him to exist; they hoped that he didn't exist… but I believe they doubted.

I asked Jean why she thought that her parent's hadn't simply concluded what to them should have been the obvious thing; that Alfie was simply a figment of her imagination:

> I think the incident with the dirt on the carpet had an effect. Probably they really did believe that I had snuck outside, but when I was so insistent it wasn't me, maybe they were like 99 percent sure, but not 100 percent. I think they could see that I was sincere when I told them it was Alfie, and that bothered them a little.

Alfie would often accompany Jean when she went out, and often walked to school with her. However, whenever other kids showed up on the sidewalk he would go quiet, refusing to speak.

> I don't know whether he just wanted to observe – he
> would stare at the other kids very intently when they
> were speaking – or whether he couldn't speak... you
> know... like if he'd spoke they would have heard him,
> even though they couldn't see him.

Once again we see this curious combination of both interaction and lack of interaction with the physical world. All QCCs seem to demonstrate this, and yet not all of them demonstrate it in the same way.

As we have seen, some QCCs will disappear completely when people other than the principal experient enter the room. Others will stay visible to the experient, but remain invisible to everyone else. Some QCCs will talk to their earthly companion when others are present, but only the experient will hear them. Others will remain silent in the presence of others, generating the possibility that if they spoke they would be heard by anyone in the vicinity. According to Jean, Alfie appeared completely 'solid'. 'He looked perfectly normal in every way... he didn't appear like a ghost, or anything; you know... semi-transparent or insubstantial.'

In fact, this characteristic of QCCs was common throughout all types. Rarely did an experient say to me that their quasi-corporeal companion looked 'like a ghost'. They always appear completely and absolutely *solid*.

I wanted to know about the time Jean believed she may have visited 'Alfie's world', as I'd never heard any other experients make such a claim. This aspect of her story was extremely interesting indeed.

> One time, just before Alfie's visits stopped, I noticed
> something weird. There was this time when we heard
> Mom coming up the stairs, and Alfie looked alarmed.
> He ran over towards the foot of my bed and
> disappeared.
>
> I didn't think anything about it at the time, but later I
> wondered just why he'd done that. Why didn't he just
> disappear where he stood? I also couldn't figure out
> why he'd disappeared at all. When he walked me to

school he didn't disappear when the other kids came around, he just stopped talking. Why couldn't he have done the same when my Mom came into the room?

The next time Alfie came, he appeared just where he'd disappeared the previous time; by the bed. I started to call this spot Alfie's secret door, because it was like there was a door there he could go through into somewhere else – I just couldn't see it.

Inevitably, one supposes, Jean came to wonder whether she could see that door or contact Alfie through it. She would stare at the place by the bed, wishing him to appear. It never worked. On other occasions she would shout 'through the door' – or at least, the spot where she believed this invisible door was – in the hope that Alfie would hear her. That didn't work either. However, there was one occasion when she believes that she may – she can't be certain – have journeyed through the door to the other side:

I had been playing with my dolls while lying on my bedroom floor, and at some point I must have fallen asleep. I can't remember feeling tired, and have no recollection of going into a slumber, but I must have done. Then I had this weird dream, and I thought, 'This is where Alfie lives.'

I asked Jean why she thought that, and what her 'weird dream' had to do with her assumption that she'd actually visited Alfie's strange world and not just had a 'weird dream' *per se.*

I think it was because I'd fallen asleep with my head near his secret door. I hadn't meant to do this, I just did. Somehow I just had this feeling that because I'd fallen asleep with my head in that spot I'd somehow got to see what it was like where he lived.

This, of course, leads us to consider some extremely interesting questions which we'll come to momentarily. At this juncture, however, we'll let Jean take up her narrative and relate to us just what she saw when she enjoyed her tantalising glimpse of what may indeed have been 'Alfie's world':

The first thing I noticed was that it was night... or at least it was very dark. It must have been night, I suppose, because I was outside. I felt uncomfortable, because I was sitting right in the middle of a road. There was a line running down the centre, and it was a well-kept blacktop road. It was shining, as if it had been raining, but I also remember that the road didn't feel wet.

There was nothing on either side of the road that I could see, but I just got this feeling of a flat, wide-open expanse. I'm sure there was just grassy fields to the left and the right, although it was too dark to see them.

In the distance I could see what looked like two big hills or mountains. The road seemed to go directly in between them. Because it was dark they were just like silhouettes, but I knew what they were because their outlines were all rugged and jagged. The sky was pinky-purple in colour, and I remember thinking how nice it looked. There were clouds, too, and they were pinky-purple – just a lighter shade – but they didn't seem to be moving.

The strange thing about this place was the silence. I was outdoors, and yet I could hear absolutely *nothing*; not a bird, not a cricket...not even a breeze. It was like sitting in the middle of a still photograph, only it was three-dimensional.

The other thing I remember was getting this overwhelming feeling that I was the only living thing for miles and miles. I felt really peaceful. I didn't feel threatened, because somehow I knew that there was nothing around to threaten me. I was on my own.

I asked Jean if this didn't mitigate against the idea that she'd visited Alfie's world. If there was no one there, how could that be the place where Alfie lived?

But there *were* people there... lots of them. Somehow I knew they were there, but just a great distance away. I could sense Alfie and lots of others, milling around, but they were miles away.

Jean also recalls that although the mountains were 'way in the distance', she felt that if she'd stretched out her hands she could have touched them. They were far away, she says, and yet simultaneously very near.

At this juncture Jean returned to her 'normal' world, but she feels that she then slept for some time before waking up.

On the surface, it seems that there is little about Jean's vision that we can hang our metaphorical hat on. However, there are some peculiar features of this strange landscape that demand our attention.

Firstly, in some respects this 'world' of Alfie's was similar to our own. There was earth beneath her feet, mountains, sky, clouds and even a tarred road with a central line painted upon it. Although it was dark, she could also see colours that she recognised. The perception of colour inevitably demands the presence of light, even though Jean doesn't mention stars or the moon. Perhaps most oddly, the blacktop road implies that Alfie's world was to some degree industrialised and blessed with technology. A tarred a road can only – at least in our world – be created by creating tar and then melting it, after which it has to be laid. The presence of a painted centre line also implies traffic – almost certainly mechanised.

But there are differences between our world and Alfie's, too. Jean's senses were heightened, for example. She could 'sense' the presence of grass, even though she could not see it, and 'sense' the presence of people, although by her own testimony she could also 'sense' that they were 'miles away'. In some respects, her physical and mental senses seemed to function better in Alfie's world than in our own.

And yet other senses were distorted. She seemed unable to detect movement. It was, as you will recall, as if she was sitting in the middle of a still photograph, only it was three-dimensional. Her perception of space and distance were also distorted. Even though visually the mountains appeared to be in the distance, she had the strange feeling that if she were to stretch out her hand she could have touched them.

Alfie's world is like ours, then, but not quite the same.

Of course, our entire hypothesis rests on the assumption that Jean really did visit Alfie's world, and that she wasn't simply experiencing a bizarre dream. There is a postscript to this story, however, which indicates that she may indeed have paid a short visit to the dimension inhabited by her quasi-corporeal companion.

The next time Alfie visited Jean, which to the best of her recollection was the following day, she told him about her experience. His reaction unsettled her:

He looked shocked when I told him. His eyes opened wide and he just stared at me intently. Then he just disappeared. He didn't come back for another week or so, and I knew inside that I shouldn't try to talk to him about my experience again because he wouldn't like it.

In the final analysis we cannot really be sure of anything except the fact that Jean, for a few years, enjoyed the presence of a QCC called Alfie – whoever or whatever he may have been. We cannot be certain that she travelled to Alfie's world – but the thought that she may have done is an intriguing one.

Chapter thirty-two

Curses and blessings

The question of whether QCCs are 'a problem' or not is a vexing one, and can be approached from a number of different perspectives.

In times past, researchers argued that the phenomenon of 'imaginary' friends was relatively rare, and that it probably heralded the onset of some sort of emotional disturbance, albeit minor. One psychologist I spoke to said, 'We used to see this as a red flag.'

Things have changed, however. Now, the majority of experts seem to believe that the presence of an 'imaginary friend' is at worst not beneficial in any tangible way, and at best may even play a necessary role in the cognitive development of the young experient. That the old 'Danger! Danger!' view has largely passed should be counted as a blessing.

Many psychologists now recognise that the presence of a QCC can have positive benefits in the life of the experient. One of the common 'positives' now heralded is that the QCC can provide much-needed companionship for the child, enabling the youngster to become creative and try out 'new ways' of playing games and enjoying recreational activities. While its nice to see experts take such a positive view, its disturbing that their perception of just why having a QCC is beneficial is only a hair's-breadth away from the old (and now discredited) idea that it is only 'lonely children' who have such companions.

It is also now recognised that the presence of an 'imaginary friend' can help the young experient develop much-needed social skills, such as the ability to hold meaningful conversations with their peers. This is common sense, really. Whether the 'playmate' is real or imaginary, social interaction with them cannot be a bad thing if the end result is a heightened ability to communicate.

Some researchers have suggested that QCCs are really a 'sounding board' upon which experients can 'bounce off' or 'test' their thoughts and feelings before trying them out on 'real' people. Personally, I don't think that this idea flies well.

Firstly, during my research I never once came across an experient who, consciously or subconsciously, indicated to me that their QCC could be used to test-run ideas to see whether they were socially acceptable. Secondly, QCCs often portray habits, thoughts and ideas that, while not socially objectionable, are at odds with the feelings of the experient. If the QCC is truly imaginary, and is generated within the cerebellum of the experient, then the ideas expressed by the QCC must also have come from within the mind of the experient too. This means that the experient must be in some way externalising already latent notions and then getting the QCC to 'feed them back' to the experient who then adopts them. Try as I might, I could find no one who was prepared to postulate this concept, even though I can't see any way to escape it if their hypothesis is correct.

Another idea which is gaining increasing popularity is the notion that children invent QCCs so that they can 'control' them, and thus learn how to manipulate or control 'real' people more efficiently. Well, you can't have it both ways. If QCCs are really 'sounding boards' that can let children see whether their ideas and feelings will be accepted in the real world before they are adopted and carried out, this implies that the QCC actually exercises an amount of control over the child, *not* the other way round.

Sometimes researchers suggest that the presence of a QCC allows the experient to have a 'private world' from which adults are excluded. There may be a degree of truth in this, but not much. In my experience, experients have little or no desire to keep adults out of the 'world' they enjoy with their QCC. If anything, the opposite is true. Experients become angry and frustrated when their parents refuse to acknowledge the existence of the QCC and allow he/she/it to interact with the 'real' world the parents inhabit. It is usually the parents who want to push the QCC away from the 'real' world, and not the child.

It has also been suggested that QCCs are simply whipping posts; imaginary children whom experients can blame for their own bad behaviour. Again, my experience while interviewing experients did not bear this out. The vast majority of experients were protective towards their QCCs, and, as at least two testimonies show, became quite irate at the notion that they could have passed the buck on to their QCC for their own misdemeanours. In one case, the experient actually invented a *truly* fictitious personage to blame for his naughtiness as blaming his QCC would have precipitated too much angst and guilt.

In the final analysis, I think it is safe to say that QCCs, whatever or whoever they are, are not really problematical and do not pose a threat to the experients they interact with. However, there is another potential problem that must be addressed, although it is one rarely spoken about.

Because we know so little about the true nature of QCCs it follows that we also know very little about their agenda, if indeed they have one. This poses a number of intriguing questions. Just why do QCCs present themselves to experients? What, if anything, do they hope to gain? What compels them to visit our earthly dimension in the way that they do?

Superficially there is a strong case to be put forward that QCCs are harmless. If indeed they do have an agenda, then it doesn't seem to be one that poses any tangible threats to those of us who have interacted with them. But this is merely a hypothesis built upon experience and we cannot be certain. Let's take a look at an analogy: Supposing a complete stranger said to a parent, 'I have a cage at home with an animal in it, and I'd like to put your child inside that cage so that it can interact with the animal'. The first question would undoubtedly be, 'What sort of animal is it?' A hamster, bunny rabbit or goldfish in a bowl would pose no threat to a child, but a cougar, wolf or bear most certainly would. Parents need to have a degree of certainty when it comes to exposing their children to potentially dangerous situations. They need to know what environment the child will be entering, and just what that environment contains. The problem is that although QCCs *seem* to be essentially harmless, we do not *know* that for certain. It is just possible that interaction with quasi-corporeal companions does precipitate a degree of harm within the experient, but that such harm is subtle and not immediately visible.

Do I believe that this is the case? No. My own feeling is that QCCs are almost certainly harmless. They aren't dangerous; they are merely strange.

Chapter thirty-three

The fear of death

James Boswell once recalled a conversation he had with that great wit Dr Samuel Johnson. The subject at hand was whether it was natural for human beings to fear death or not. Boswell wasn't entirely sure, and thus solicited Johnson's opinion on the matter:

> 'I mentioned to him that I had seen the execution of several convicts at Tyburn, and that none of them seemed to be under any concern."

> Johnson, typically, replied that, 'Most of them, Sir, have never thought at all.'

> 'But is not the fear of death natural to a man?' enquired Boswell.

> 'So much so, Sir, that the whole of life is but keeping away the thoughts of it', retorted the Doctor.

According to Boswell, Johnson then, 'in a low and earnest tone, talked of his meditating upon the awful hour of his own dissolution, and in what manner he should conduct himself upon that occasion.'

> 'I know not', said Johnson, 'whether I should wish to have a friend by me, or have it all between God and myself'.

There is much to be had from Johnson's words, and just possibly some insight into the purpose, if any, that quasi-corporeal companions may serve.

It was not so much the fear of dying that troubled the Doctor, but rather the fear of dying *alone*. Whether Johnson wished to have a friend present with him as he shuffled off this mortal coil, or simply the presence of his Creator, he hadn't worked out; but he wanted *someone* there.

Human beings are fragile and untrustworthy. Most of us try to lead a reasonably decent life, but none of us succeed perfectly. All of us, I would venture, have at some juncture badly let down a friend – failed to be there for them when they needed us. And yet, the need for perfectly trustworthy companions is not lessened by their scarcity any more than a paucity of food assuages hunger. Just the opposite, in fact – it makes the need all the more acute.

Quasi-corporeal companions are enigmatic. Their bizarre behaviour puzzles us, and yet they never let us down. Perhaps from a very young age there is a desire latent in many of us to possess a 'special friend' that we can truly trust, even if they can never be fully understood. Perhaps this is the friend that Johnson may have wanted with him when he passed away, and the friend that introduces him or herself to us when we are yet of tender years and far from the shadow of death.

This does not explain, of course, how the object of our desire can be real in any meaningful sense purely because we wish for it. This, too, is merely another part of the enigma of quasi-corporeal companions.

Chapter thirty-four

Conclusions

In her story *The Life of Ma Parker*, Katherine Mansfield wrote, 'Why was this stranger standing in the kitchen...? What was it all about?' A question, I would venture, that could as well spring from the lips of any QCC experient. The world we live in is a curious place, filled with wonders that we can barely comprehend. Indeed, it is this lack of comprehension that *makes* our experiences wonderful. Things that we fully understand are not wonderful at all; merely intriguing.

The world of paranormal research is one of the most satisfying landscapes we can visit, for it feeds our need not to know everything. Living in an environment where nothing is left open to debate would be boring to the extreme. There is something in the human condition that forces us to quest, to look for answers when we aren't even certain about the questions. The phenomenon of quasi-corporeal companions panders to this need most wonderfully.

In some respects we know much about QCCs. We can say that they truly exist – even if, and I do not subscribe to this notion – they are merely figments of an over-active imagination.

We know that they may take on a number of different forms, each type possessing its own personality characteristics and set of 'rules'. They are almost certainly harmless, and are probably beneficial to those who are privileged to interact with them. We also know that they possess abilities not normally found within the province of normal human life; they can appear and disappear at will, perform magical feats and change their appearance in the most bizarre fashion.

And yet, we also know very little. We may suspect that they hail from other dimensions, but testimony as to what those dimensions look like is scant indeed. We do not know whether those dimensions exist within the same time-space co-ordinates as our own, or whether they are to be found light years away on the other side of the galaxy. We do not know how QCCs travel here, or even if they 'travel' here at all in the conventional sense of the word. We do not know what there agenda is, or even if they have one. Earlier I queried whether QCCs provide anything positive to we humans when we interact with them; but what if they are not fulfilling needs of ours, but rather needs of theirs? So many questions.

There are, I think, parallels between the QCC experience and other paranormal disciplines such as the alien abduction phenomenon and the witnessing of apparitions. Millions – probably billions – of people alive today, in a multitude of different geographical locations and cultural scenarios, are witnesses to the veracity of the QCC experience. Perhaps the very commonness of the phenomenon is the reason why it has attracted so little attention. Yet, with so many eyewitnesses around to interview, there must be hope that further study can shed light on a sorely under-researched circumstance. Hope, yes, but not necessarily hope that is well-grounded.

One of the common features of paranormal research in all its aspects is the Butterfingers Rule. Researchers into the alien abduction phenomenon, the poltergeist enigma, mystery big cats *et al* know this rule well, although they may express it differently. The Butterfingers Rule has three parts to it, and they may be expressed like this:

  a) Explanations for any paranormal phenomenon will multiply proportionately to the amount of data accrued.

  b) When a satisfactory explanation for any given paranormal phenomenon is seemingly found, new data will immediately present itself to make the explanation redundant.

  c) The harder a researchers tries to arrive at an explanation for any given phenomenon, the more complex the phenomenon will become and the more elusive the answer will seem to be.

When someone tries to hang on to a lump of butter, the faster it squeezes through their fingers and eludes their grasp. The harder we try, the less successful we are. Paranormal researchers who have not encountered this rule in some shape or form can only be apprentices to the craft and virginal in their experience.

Why, then, do we bother to research at all if reaching a successful conclusion is essentially a useless task? There are two reasons, I think.

Firstly, there is the old adage of Alexander Pope, found in his *Essay on Man*, that 'Hope springs eternal in the human breast'. We humans cannot help ourselves. When there is something to be striven for, then we strive. It is an autonomic action, essentially unstoppable.

Secondly, almost all the paranormal researchers I know sincerely believe that they are searching for answers. Enigmatically, however, they only ever find them when what seemed to be a paranormal phenomenon turns out to be nothing of the kind. I may find an answer to a haunting when the haunting turns out to be some wag dressed up in a sheet. I may find an explanation for a UFO sighting when what seemed to be an alien spacecraft proved to be a dustbin lid suspended from a washing line. We are only allowed answers to seemingly paranormal phenomena in individual cases, and the answers we find speak only of human ingenuity, and nothing of the reality or otherwise of the phenomenon. Deep down we all know this, and yet we march on unabashed. Why? Because the search for answers is not what really drives us at all; what we hunger for is the experience. It is, to coin a phrase, the thrill of the chase that excites us, not the capturing of the prey.

For these reasons and more I hold no confidence that the QCC phenomenon will ever be solved successfully. We may come to know more about the individual bits, but nothing about the sum of the parts. Those who would like to investigate the QCC phenomenon should be aware that they, too, will be subjected to the tri-part Butterfingers Rule.

Yesterday I interviewed a young child who has a QCC called Derek. Derek is a young boy who walks with a stick because of his 'bad leg'. He almost always carries an orange in his hand, although Steven says that on the rare occasions he doesn't there is always a huge bulge in the pocket of his shorts which indicates that the orange is still in Derek's possession.

Who is Derek? I know not, but something deep inside testifies to me that he is not entirely insubstantial. He comes from a hidden place, stays awhile, and then returns to the abode from whence he came. Derek likes chips, but he doesn't like fish. He likes to read comics, but not books without pictures. Derek appears regularly, but not on Sundays. On Sunday, you see, he has to go to Pointy's. Steven does not know what or who Pointy is, as Derek refuses to discuss the matter with him.

Some things, it seems, are destined to remain secrets. It is the way of things, and I have no complaint.

But I reserve the right to wonder.

Index

STILL ON THE TRACK OF UNKNOWN ANIMALS

The Centre for Fortean Zoology, or CFZ, is a non profit-making organisation founded in 1992 with the aim of being a clearing house for information, and coordinating research into mystery animals around the world.

We also study out of place animals, rare and aberrant animal behaviour, and Zooform Phenomena; little-understood "things" that appear to be animals, but which are in fact nothing of the sort, and not even alive (at least in the way we understand the term).

Not only are we the biggest organisation of our type in the world, but - or so we like to think - we are the best. We are certainly the only truly global cryptozoological research organisation, and we carry out our investigations using a strictly scientific set of guidelines. We are expanding all the time and looking to recruit new members to help us in our research into mysterious animals and strange creatures across the globe.

Why should you join us? Because, if you are genuinely interested in trying to solve the last great mysteries of Mother Nature, there is nobody better than us with whom to do it.

We publish a journal *Animals & Men*. Each issue contains nearly 100 pages packed with news, articles, letters, research papers, field reports, and even a gossip column! The magazine is Royal Octavo in format with a full colour cover. You also have access to one of the world's largest collections of resource material dealing with cryptozoology and allied disciplines, and people from the CFZ membership regularly take part in fieldwork and expeditions around the world.

The CFZ is managed by a board of trustees, with a non-profit making trust registered with HM Government Stamp Office. The board of trustees is supported by a Permanent Directorate of full and part-time staff, and advised by a Consultancy Board of specialists - many of whom are world-renowned experts in their particular field. We have regional representatives across the UK, the USA, and many other parts of the world, and are affiliated with other organisations whose aims and protocols mirror our own.

You'll find that the people at the CFZ are friendly and approachable. We have a thriving forum on the website which is the hub of an ever-growing electronic community. You will soon find your feet. Many members of the CFZ Permanent Directorate started off as ordinary members, and now work full-time chasing monsters around the world.

Write to us, e-mail us, or telephone us. The list of future projects on the website is not exhaustive. If you have a good idea for an investigation, please tell us. We may well be able to help.

We are always looking for volunteers to join us. If you see a project that interests you, do not hesitate to get in touch with us. Under certain circumstances we can help provide funding for your trip. If you look on the future projects section of the website, you can see some of the projects that we have pencilled in for the next few years.

In 2003 and 2004 we sent three-man expeditions to Sumatra looking for Orang-Pendek - a semi-legendary bipedal ape. The same three went to Mongolia in 2005. All three members started off merely subscribers to the CFZ magazine. Next time it could be you!

We have no magic sources of income. All our funds come from donations, membership fees, and sales of our publications and merchandise. We are always looking for corporate sponsorship, and other sources of revenue. If you have any ideas for fund-raising please let us know. However, unlike other cryptozoological organisations in the past, we do not live in an intellectual ivory tower. We are not afraid to get our hands dirty, and furthermore we are not one of those organisations where the membership have to raise money so that a privileged few can go on expensive foreign trips. Our research teams, both in the UK and abroad, consist of a mixture of experienced and inexperienced personnel. We are truly a community, and work on the premise that the benefits of CFZ membership are open to all.

Reports of our investigations are published on our website as soon as they are available. Preliminary reports are posted within days of the project finishing.

Each year we publish a 200 page yearbook containing research papers and expedition reports too long to be printed in the journal. We freely circulate our information to anybody who asks for it.

We have a thriving YouTube channel, CFZtv, which has well over two hundred self-made documentaries, lecture appearances, and episodes of our monthly webTV show. We have a daily online magazine, which has over a million hits each year.

From 2000—2016 we held our annual convention - the Weird Weekend. It went on hiatus because of the illness of several of the major personnel and the eventual death of one of them. But we plan to bring it back soon. It is three days of lectures, workshops, and excursions. But most importantly it is a chance for members of the CFZ to meet each other, and to talk with the members of the permanent directorate in a relaxed and informal setting and preferably with a pint of beer in one hand. Since 2006 - the Weird Weekend has been bigger and better and held in the idyllic rural location of Woolsery in North Devon.

Since relocating to North Devon in 2005 we have become ever more closely involved with other community organisations, and we hope that this trend

will continue. We have also worked closely with Police Forces across the UK as consultants for animal mutilation cases, and we intend to forge closer links with the coastguard and other community services. We want to work closely with those who regularly travel into the Bristol Channel, so that if the recent trend of exotic animal visitors to our coastal waters continues, we can be out there as soon as possible.

Apart from having been the only Fortean Zoological organisation in the world to have consistently published material on all aspects of the subject for over a decade, we have achieved the following concrete results:

• Disproved the myth relating to the headless so-called sea-serpent carcass of Durgan beach in Cornwall 1975

• Disproved the story of the 1988 puma skull of Lustleigh Cleave

- Carried out the only in-depth research ever into the mythos of the Cornish Owlman.
- Made the first records of a tropical species of lamprey
- Made the first records of a luminous cave gnat larva in Thailand
- Discovered a possible new species of British mammal - the beech marten
- In 1994-6 carried out the first archival fortean zoological survey of Hong Kong
- In the year 2000, CFZ theories were confirmed when a new species of lizard was added to the British List
- Identified the monster of Martin Mere in Lancashire as a giant wels catfish
- Expanded the known range of Armitage's skink in the Gambia by 80%
- Obtained photographic evidence of the remains of Europe's largest known pike
- Carried out the first ever in-depth study of the ninki-nanka
- Carried out the first attempt to breed Puerto Rican cave snails in captivity
- Were the first European explorers to visit the `lost valley` in Sumatra
- Published the first ever evidence for a new tribe of pygmies in Guyana
- Published the first evidence for a new species of caiman in Guyana
- Filmed unknown creatures on a monster-haunted lake in Ireland for the first time

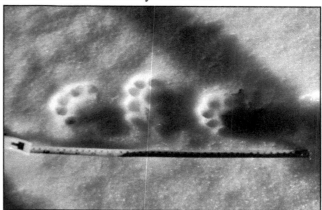

- Had a sighting of orang pendek in Sumatra in 2009
- Found leopard hair, subsequently identified by DNA analysis, from rural North Devon in 2010
- Brought back hairs which appear to be from an unknown primate in Sumatra
- Published some of the best evidence ever for the almasty in southern Russia

CFZ Expeditions and Investigations include:

- 1998 Puerto Rico, Florida, Mexico (Chupacabras)
- 1999 Nevada (Bigfoot)
- 2000 Thailand (Naga)
- 2002 Martin Mere (Giant catfish)
- 2002 Cleveland (Wallaby mutilation)
- 2003 Bolam Lake (BHM Reports)

- 2003 Sumatra (Orang Pendek)
- 2003 Texas (Bigfoot; giant snapping turtles)
- 2004 Sumatra (Orang Pendek; cigau, a sabre-toothed cat)
- 2004 Illinois (Black panthers; cicada swarm)
- 2004 Texas (Mystery blue dog)
- Loch Morar (Monster)
- 2004 Puerto Rico (Chupacabras; carnivorous cave snails)
- 2005 Belize (Affiliate expedition for hairy dwarfs)
- 2005 Loch Ness (Monster)
- 2005 Mongolia (Allghoi Khorkhoi aka Mongolian death worm)

- 2006 Gambia (Gambo - Gambian sea monster , Ninki Nanka and Armitage's skink
- 2006 Llangorse Lake (Giant pike, giant eels)
- 2006 Windermere (Giant eels)
- 2007 Coniston Water (Giant eels)
- 2007 Guyana (Giant anaconda, didi, water tiger)
- 2008 Russia (Almasty)
- 2009 Sumatra (Orang pendek)
- 2009 Republic of Ireland (Lake Monster)
- 2010 Texas (Blue Dogs)
- 2010 India (Mande Burung)
- 2011 Sumatra (Orang-pendek)
- 2012 Sumatra (Orang Pendek)
- 2014 Tasmania (Thylacine)
- 2015 Tasmania (Thylacine)
- 2016 Tasmania (Thylacine)
- 2017 Tasmania (Thylacine)
- 2018 Tajikistan (Gul)
- 2020 Forest of Dean (Lynx)

For details of current membership fees, current expeditions and investigations, and voluntary posts within the CFZ that need your help, please do not hesitate to contact us.

The Centre for Fortean Zoology,
Myrtle Cottage,
Woolfardisworthy,
Bideford, North Devon
EX39 5QR

Telephone 01237 431413
Fax+44 (0)7006-074-925
eMail info@cfz.org.uk

Websites:

www.cfz.org.uk
www.weirdweekend.org

HOW TO START A PUBLISHING EMPIRE

Unlike most mainstream publishers, we have a non-commercial remit, and our mission state-ment claims that "we publish books because they deserve to be published, not because we think that we can make money out of them". Our motto is the Latin Tag *Pro bona causa faci-mus* (we do it for good reason), a slogan taken from a children's book *The Case of the Silver Egg* by the late Desmond Skirrow.

WIKIPEDIA: "The first book published was in 1988. *Take this Brother may it Serve you Well* was a guide to Beatles bootlegs by Jonathan Downes. It sold quite well, but was hampered by very poor production values, being photocopied, and held together by a plastic clip binder.

In 1988 A5 clip binders were hard to get hold of, so the publishers took A4 binders and cut them in half with a hacksaw. It now reaches surprisingly high prices second hand.

The production quality improved slightly over the years, and after 1999 all the books produced were ringbound with laminated colour covers. In 2004, however, they signed an agreement with Lightning Source, and all books are now produced perfect bound, with full colour co-vers."

Until 2010 all our books, the majority of which are/were on the subject of mystery animals and allied disciplines, were published by `CFZ Press`, the publishing arm of the Centre for Fortean Zoology (CFZ), and we urged our readers and followers to draw a discreet veil over the books that we published that were completely off topic to the CFZ.

However, in 2010 we decided that enough was enough and launched a second imprint, `Fortean Words` which aims to cover a wide range of non animal-related esoteric subjects. Other imprints will be launched as and when we feel like it, however the basic ethos of the company remains the same: Our job is to publish books and magazines that we feel are worth publishing, whether or not they are going to sell. Money is, after all - as my dear old Mama once told me - a rather vulgar subject, and she would be rolling in her grave if she thought that her eldest son was somehow in `trade`.

Luckily, so far our tastes have turned out not to be that rarified after all, and we have sold far more books than anyone ever thought that we would, so there is a moral in there somewhere...

Jon Downes,
Woolsery, North Devon
July 2010

CFZ PRESS

CFZ Press is our flagship imprint, featuring a wide range of intelligently written and lavishly illustrated books on cryptozoology and the quirkier aspects of Natural History.

CFZ Classics is a new venture for us. There are many seminal works that are either unavailable today, or not available with the production values which we would like to see. So, following the old adage that if you want to get something done do it yourself, this is exactly what we have done.

Desiderius Erasmus Roterodamus (b. October 18th 1466, d. July 2nd 1536) said: "When I have a little money, I buy books; and if I have any left, I buy food and clothes," and we are much the same. Only, we are in the lucky position of being able to share our books with the wider world. CFZ Classics is a conduit through which we cannot just re-issue titles which we feel still have much to offer the cryptozoological and Fortean research communities of the 21st Century, but we are adding footnotes, supplementary essays, and other material where we deem it appropriate.

http://www.cfzpublishing.co.uk/

Fortean Words is a new stands for "Fortean", after anomalous phenomena, imprint covers a whole venture for us. The F in CFZ the pioneering researcher into Charles Fort. Our Fortean Words spectrum of arcane subjects from UFOs and the paranormal to folklore and urban legends. Our authors include such Fortean luminaries as Nick Redfern, Andy Roberts, and Paul Screeton. . New authors tackling new subjects will always be encouraged, and we hope that our books will continue to be as ground-breaking and popular as ever.

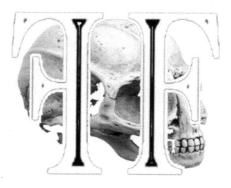

Just before Christmas third imprint, this time you guessed it from the 2011, we launched our dedicated to - let's see if title - fictional books with a Fortean or cryptozoological theme. We have published a few fictional books in the past, but now think that because of our rising reputation as publishers of quality Forteana, that a dedicated fiction imprint was the order of the day.

http://www.cfzpublishing.co.uk/